PHOTOGRAPHY
FOR THE
SCALEMODELLER

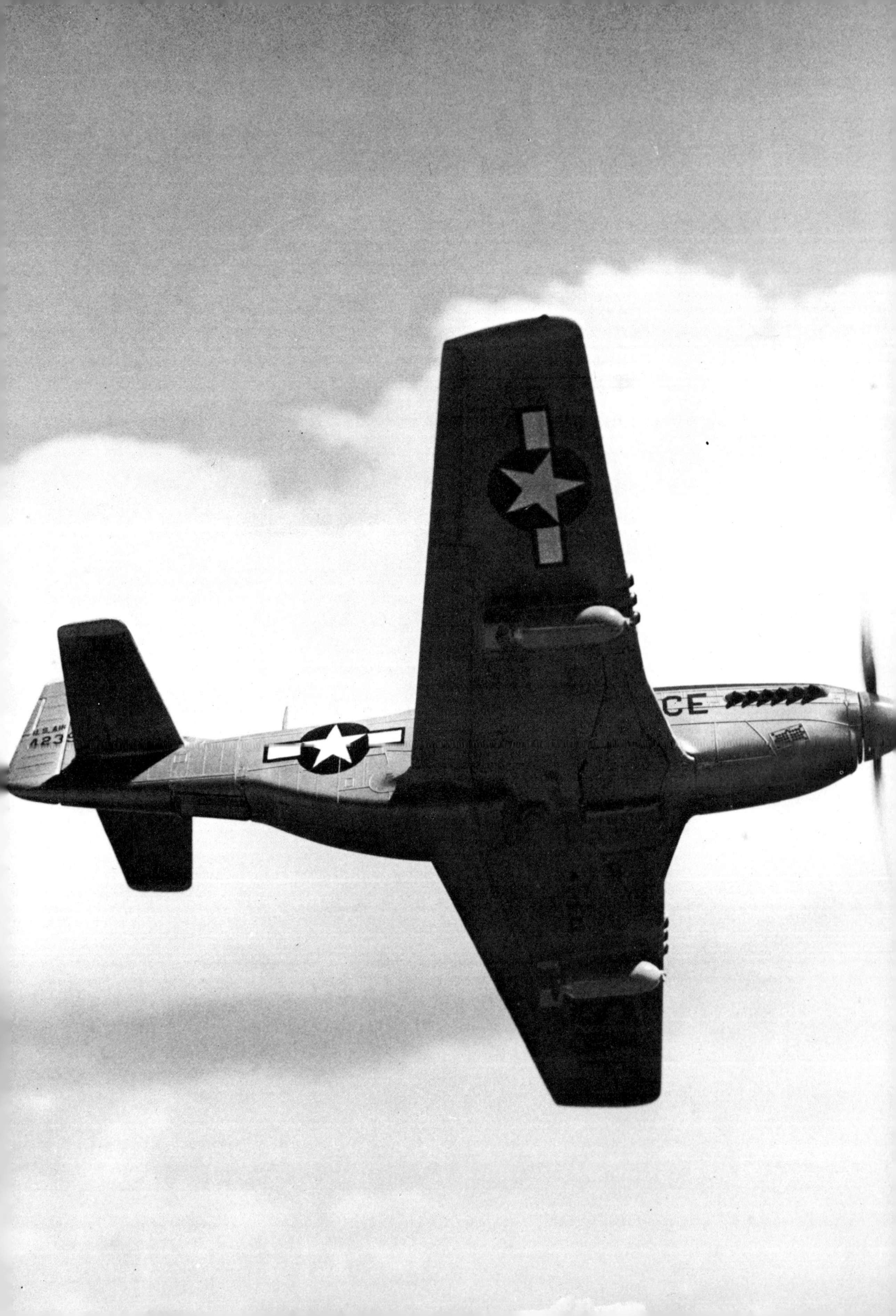
CE
U.S. AIR
423

PHOTOGRAPHY FOR THE SCALEMODELLER

by PIETER STROETHOFF

MODELBOOKS

First published 1975

MODELBOOKS
York Road, Brentford, Middlesex, England

Printed and bound by Kyodo Printing Co Ltd, Tokyo

CONTENTS

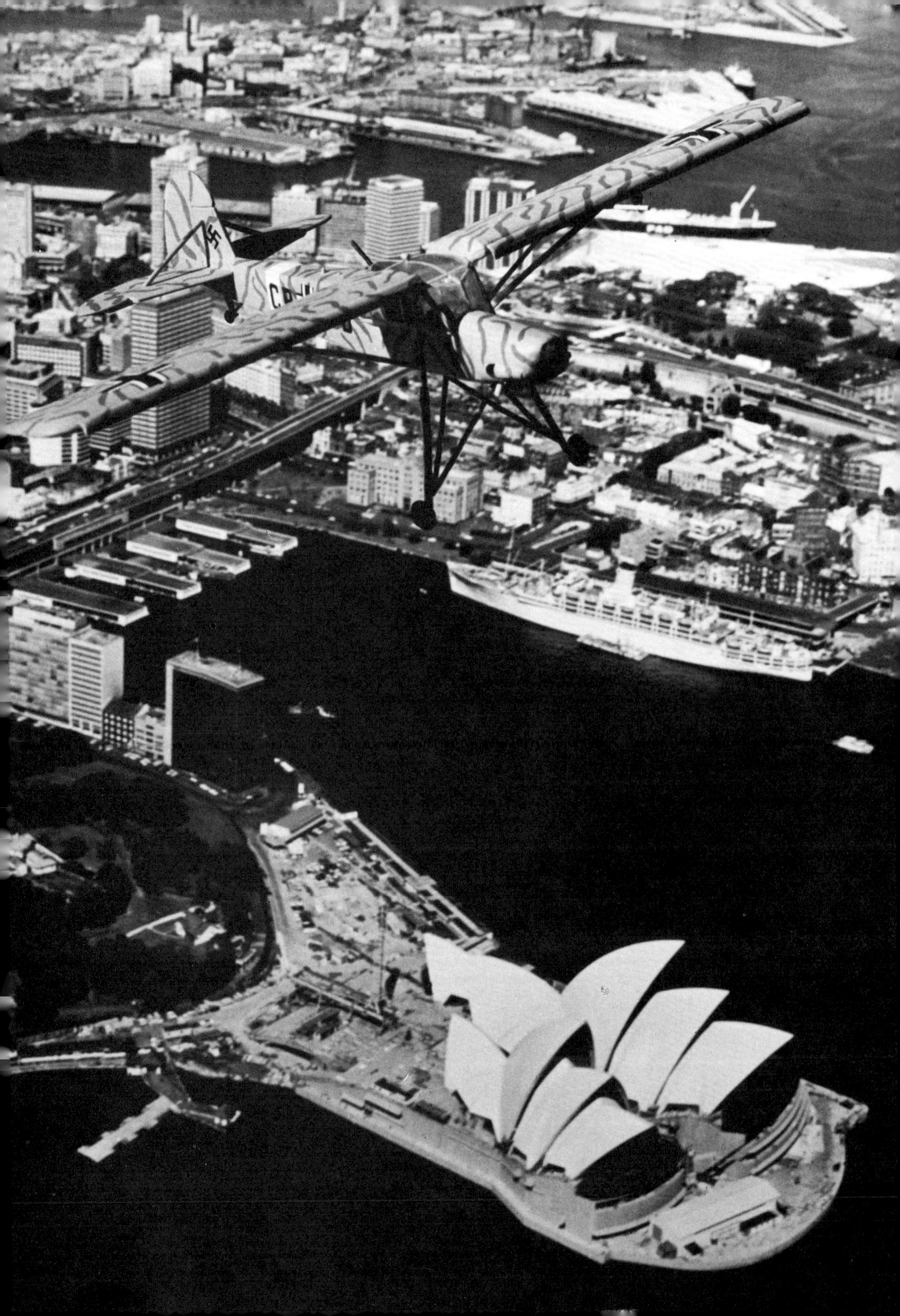

INTRODUCTION

Once upon a time there was a man who worked long hours building scale models. With painstaking care he assembled them and after he had painted them in some authentic colour scheme, they were difficult to distinguish from the real thing. Yet he was not happy. He wanted to do something better than put them in a glass case where they would be safe, or in the old shoe box with all his other models, where they were far from safe.

It is for this man that we wrote this book. Plastic models these days have reached a high standard in detailing and general appearance. They are in all aspects true replicas of the original but it is the skilled modeller who can make them more than that. Many of us verify basic outlines and details with the assistance of model magazines. We correct any apparent discrepancies, we even venture conversions. It is, however, the infinite care with which we apply the finishing touches which seems to give our model a soul, just like its full-sized counterpart has a soul. It is at this stage of creative fervour that so many of us want to complete the illusion of reality. We try to capture in a photograph the feelings our model has inspired in us. How much more pleasure we would get out of our efforts if we could make our friends believe they were looking at a print of the real thing, while it was in fact our latest model.

Here we have touched on the idea behind all the photographs in this book: deception. Our aim must be to deceive anyone looking at our prints. We are convinced that this is also about the only way to do the model the justice it deserves. All too often, alas, the pictures we produce reveal our dreams as having returned to just another model.

We hope to enable you to break this evil spell by pointing out the pitfalls, and teaching you a few tricks as we go along.

The reader will notice that most of this book is dedicated to models of aircraft. There is, of course, a very good reason for this: aircraft can be found in a wide variety of poses that would not really suit other models. Yet the principles we shall discuss here apply equally to all types of models.

Your ship, train or AFV can come to life. Some ingenuity, a lot of patience and an understanding of the theories contained in this book are all you need.

CHAPTER

1 MODEL v. REALITY

In this chapter we will try to define just what it is that makes most photographs instantly recognisable as being those of a model.

When we photograph an actual object, be it car, ship or aeroplane, we invariably do this outdoors. Consequently the sun is our main source of illumination and our object is depicted in its natural surroundings. The sun is, as far as we are concerned, only a very small pin-point type of light source, despite its enormous dimensions. The shadows it creates are of a particular kind with which we will deal in a later chapter; suffice it to say that they give outdoor photographs a special quality so that we can easily identify a photograph taken in natural sunlight. This condition needs to be very carefully duplicated for our indoor table-top settings.

Of more importance than the lighting, however, is the point from which we take our pictures. Inevitably our cameras are held somewhere in the region between our waist and eyes, depending on the type of camera we are using; our own habits play an important part in this too. There are those who will go to extraordinary lengths in their efforts to obtain special effects. Obviously the distance between camera and ground in a model setting must be in proportion with the model, and the same applies to the distance between camera and object, although admittedly this particular distance can, in real life, be varied freely, without resulting in impossible pictures. It therefore applies mainly to the lower end of the scale, where the proper distance would mean a range reduced to a mere few inches. At this point we will undoubtedly encounter our first purely technical trouble: very few cameras are equipped with a focusing mechanism that allows us to take pictures at such a short distance. These are extreme cases, but unfortunately very small models, and most of the ones reproduced at 1/72 scale fall into this group, are best photographed at such close quarters, simply because it gives the person looking at the resulting photograph the illusion of being very near the object. As the following chapter is devoted entirely to cameras and related products we shall defer until then a full discussion of the technical aspect of this problem. The task now faced, is to analyse the circumstances that lead to the person admiring our photographs forgetting his actual size and coming under the illusion that he is only the size of the model.

The relationship between observer and object is something we take for granted in real life. We accept things the way we see them, and usually they happen to be just right for our purposes. Only once in my career as a professional photographer did I succeed, unintentionally, in producing a picture of a building that possessed all the qualities of a picture of a model.

When we look at the things around us, we can roughly gauge the distance between ourselves and the object of our interest, because our eyes enable us to measure distance and to determine whether an object is large or small. We may not realize it, but we are constantly comparing our own size with that of our surroundings.

When we see an object at a certain distance, we know approximately what this distance is; not in exact terms of feet and inches (or in meters and centimeters), of course, but our brains have received so much data as a result of our eyes scanning adjacent objects, that they can compute this distance fairly accurately; so accurately in fact, that should our object be moved slightly, either away from us or directly towards us, we can tell not only in which direction the movement was, but also approximately how far. The explanation of this phenomenon is simply that we are accustomed to seeing objects in surroundings that are somehow familiar to us. Buildings, for instance, form converging lines towards vanishing points, either on the horizon, or above or below us, depending on which way we are looking. Telegraph poles appear to become progressively smaller the further away they are. It is this all too familiar perspective that helps us to relate our dimensions with those of the object.

This whole process is of course so automatic, that we are unaware of it taking place. Yet this is exactly what happens, every single moment of our waking hours.

We would be utterly confused if it were possible to see our object absolutely isolated, floating in a void with nothing to relate it to. Numerous experiments have in fact demonstrated that a light in a matt black room appears to move. Without clues we are unable to distinguish between a very large object at a great distance and an object a quarter its size at a quarter the distance. In England in 1949 a whole village spent more than an hour searching for an aeroplane that had been seen by many people crashing in a nearby swamp. The aircraft was in fact a 3ft scale model. The owner had retrieved his model, taken it home and joined in the search, without realizing what was happening. Another example is the fact that the moon always looks larger on the horizon than it does at any other point along its path. This is often, but incorrectly, attributed to refraction of the moon's light passing through dense layers of atmosphere. Photographs taken of a full moon at the horizon and also at its highest point, will produce images of exactly the same size. Besides these examples, however, a total lack of clues is something we are not very likely to encounter, unless we become actively engaged in space travel.

It is surprising how little additional information we need to make correct judgements of size and distance: walls, trees, roads, canals, even open expanses such as seas, lakes, airfields, and most important of all, clouds and sky generally, are more than adequate.

In a photograph we have lost one of the three dimensions we have come to rely upon, and it is in this two-dimensional world that things are altogether different. We will discover that with fairly limited and often improvised means we can create a fully convincing illusion of depth. Bearing in mind that a model without any surroundings is very unlikely ever to look realistic, we must determine against what background and in what general setting our model will look its most natural. Then comes the task of reproducing that particular set of surroundings.

Obviously, all we can hope for, at best, is to reach a compromise, because we have only a limited amount of space available in our studios and also because it is just not possible to build replicas of all the things that we would normally see in a photograph of a full-sized object. The very medium of photography itself, however, will ensure that our efforts are softened sufficiently to become acceptable.

Photographs taken outdoors are further characterized by the fact that modern cameras and fairly fast film make it practically impossible to depict the entire depth of our scene in all but a sharp focus. Parts of the scenery near the horizon will usually appear in a slight haze, which enhances the feeling of distance; this condition is difficult to reproduce indoors. The use of existing photographs as background eliminates many problems we would encounter should we decide to try and build the entire scene. Many dioramas are good examples of the ingenuity displayed by their makers; they never venture away from the centrepiece more than perhaps a foot, however, and never include any sky. A comparable setting built for photographic purposes would have to be very much larger. This would involve an enormous amount of quite unnecessary work.

Summing up then, we can list the shortcomings that make a photograph instantly recognisable as a photograph of a model. In order of importance they are:

1. insufficient depth of field to bring the whole of the object into focus, which in turn leads invariably to
2. a background which is very much out of focus;
3. a background which is not in proportion with whatever is in the foreground;
4. a combination of 2 and 3;
5. incorrect lighting.

CHAPTER 2

THE CAMERA

We have more or less taken for granted that anyone who has taken the step of buying this book is already the proud owner of a fairly good camera. For those who own no such luxury, or are thinking of buying a second camera specially for photographing scale models, the following examination of available equipment will help in making the right choice.

Luckily there are relatively few cameras entirely unsuitable for our purposes; these are generally the ones that cannot be focused, the so-called fixed-focus cameras. All inexpensive cameras fall into this category, and although they are quite satisfactory when used for their intended purpose e.g. taking snapshots of family outings, we can categorically declare all these unsuitable.

Box cameras might be thought to have virtually disappeared from the market, but most of the types sold by well-known film manufacturers are basically a revival of this old and familiar camera type. They have a fixed focus and only one shutter speed, with possibly a built-in arrangement for sunny and not-so-sunny weather. The old Brownie has introduced literally millions of people to photography. Indeed the author's first camera was the family Brownie, made of plywood and cardboard. I immediately made all sorts of attachments for it, in an effort to upgrade the performance. These included an oversized sunshade, also in good tradition made of cardboard, and a much smaller lens-opening, fitted over one of the two alternative openings provided by Messrs Eastman. And indeed, by using a faster film to compensate for the loss of light caused by the smaller aperture, the quality of my pictures improved dramatically.

Today's equivalents have changed to 35mm film; they are much smaller and easier to handle and are usually equipped with numerous fairly sophisticated refinements, such as flash light sockets and beautifully bright view finders. The narrower 35mm film is of course very economical and its introduction has brought colour photography within reach of many more people; much improved colour film material and very much better printing services have played their part in making colour photography more attractive.

In this book we are not really trying to make a distinction between what is better suited for colour or black and white. Colour photography involves the use of coloured backgrounds, and our lights would have to be of the type known as photofloods (3400°K) or tungsten (3200°K). Both of these are much whiter than ordinary light bulbs, which give a comparatively red light. The advantage with colour is that, having taken our pictures, we have no further worries; either we shoot on reversal film, which results in mounted transparencies, ready for projection, or we use negative film. Both these films are sent to one of the many colour laboratories to be processed by experts, who will also make prints from our negatives.

Black and white is much simpler where the settings are concerned, but almost always we will want to do our own processing and printing. This in turn will mean an extra outlay of capital, not to mention the encroachment on precious floor space, especially in flats or home units. Much depends therefore on how each individual is already equipped.

Irrespective of our choice of film, however, it is the camera that will be the critical factor. Bigger cameras using 120 film are less suitable than 35mm SLR cameras; we have seen how a good depth of field is of vital importance. An optical system with a short focal length (35 or 50mm, as found on 35mm cameras), has just this as one of its main characteristics. Bigger cameras have of necessity longer lenses; working at the same relative opening, longer lenses have a much shallower depth of field than their shorter brethren. Lenses on technical cameras can be stopped down to f/45, thus offsetting some of the disadvantage of their longer focal length. In this field we can therefore include lenses of up to and including 180mm on our list of useful items.

In these three photographs the distance between camera and object was so chosen that in each case the image filled the entire negative.

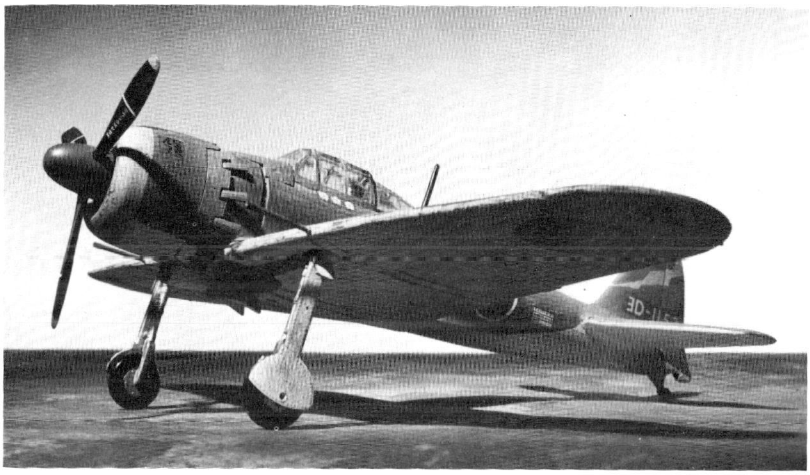

Lens 35 mm (wide angle); distance 40 cm. 1〉

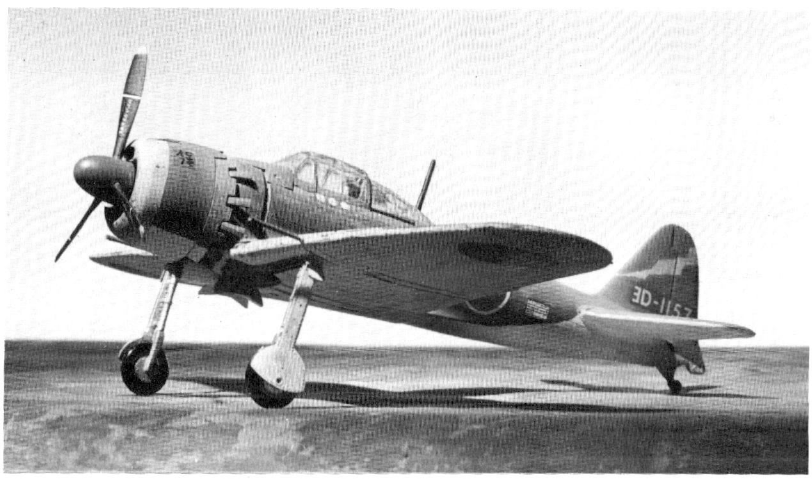

Lens 50 mm (standard); distance 65 cm. 2〉

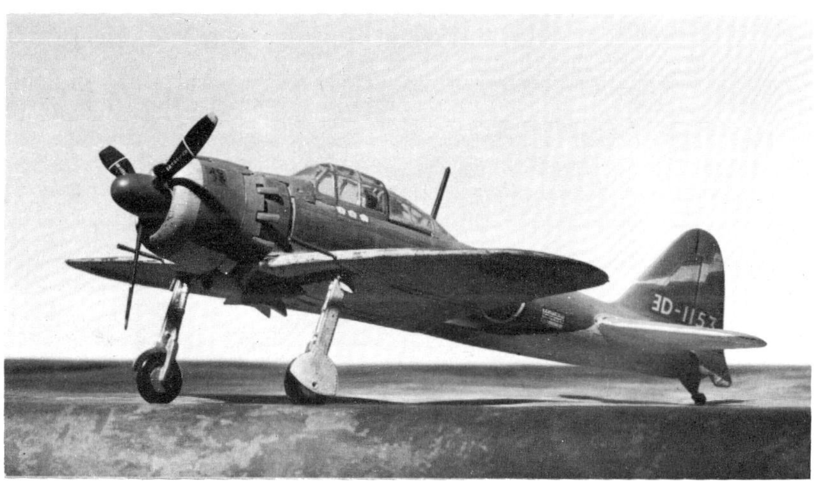

Lens 135 mm (telephoto); distance 160 cm. 3〉

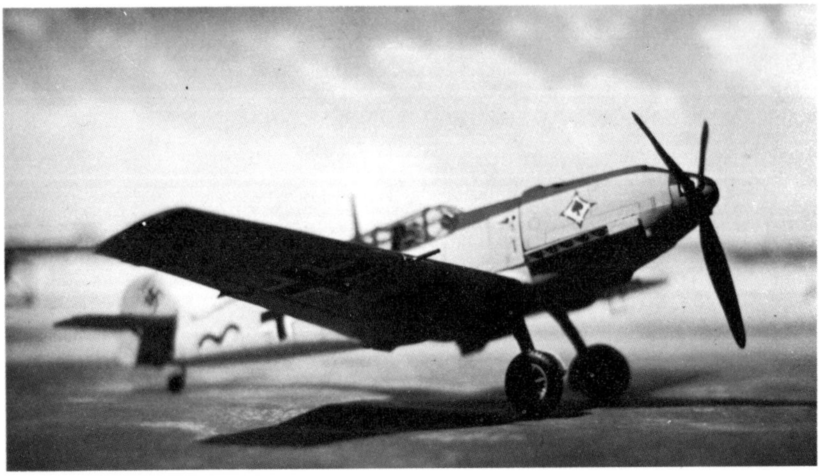

Lens wide open - depth of field insufficient to bring the model into good focus.

4

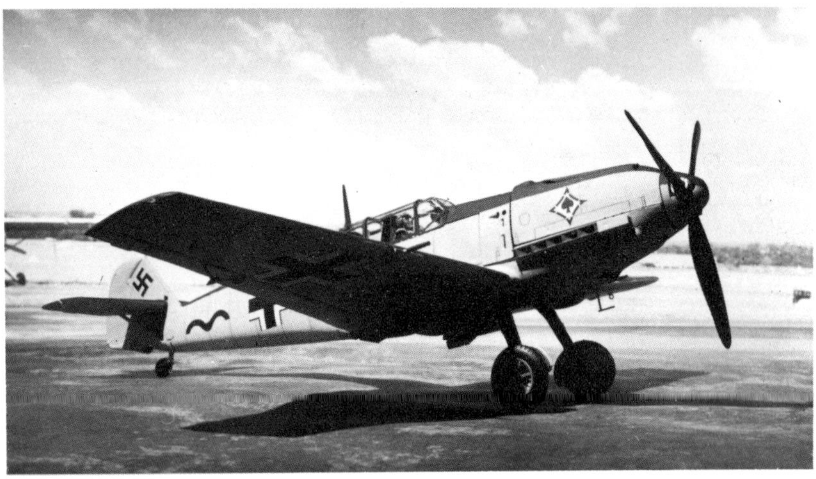

Same setting as fig. 4; lens closed to smallest available opening - good depth of field.

5

We must remember, however, that depth of field depends not on focal length and f-stop alone; the distance at which we have focused our camera is of even greater importance. The nearer we focus, the less depth of field we will get, even with a fully stopped-down lens. All this can be clearly demonstrated with formulas and a lot of paperwork, but that would be outside the scope of this book.

A small model is best photographed with a small camera, using the shortest lens we can lay our hands on; always close the diaphragm to the smallest opening possible, which is either f/16 or f/22 on 35mm cameras. Large models, such as flying ones, built for Radio Control or Control Line, can be tackled with either that same small camera or with a bigger 120 camera, also known as 2¼" square, 2¼" x 3¼" or the new 'ideal format' of 55mm x 70mm. Because the object is so much larger, we have to take our pictures from a greater distance, so counteracting to some extent the shallow depth of field inherent in longer lenses. The still larger technical camera, using sheet film of up to 4" x 5", comes into its own where a bigger model is involved. The longer focal length of the lens used, say 180mm, forces us to stay away even further; together with the smaller stop of f/45, we can obtain very good results.

It is of the utmost importance that we place the vertical background as close to the model as the conditions permit, taking into consideration such factors as correct scale and perspective and making sure the model does not throw shadows on it.

The effect of different lenses on our per-

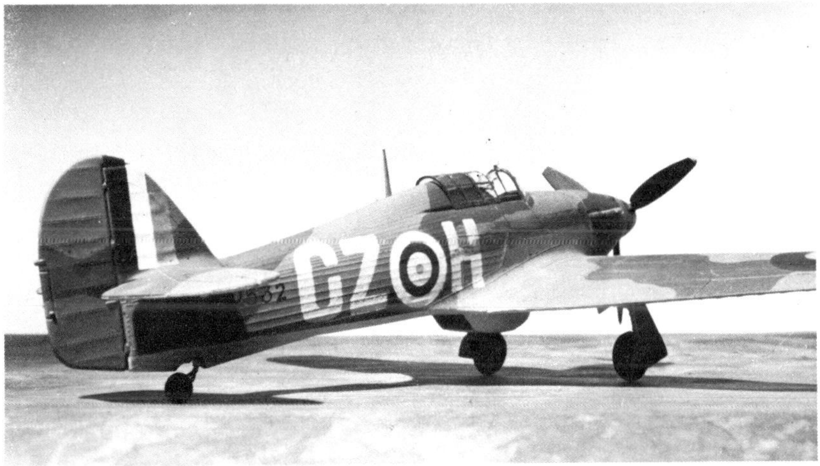

Short lens (wide angle) used too close to model - tail seems too big.

6〉

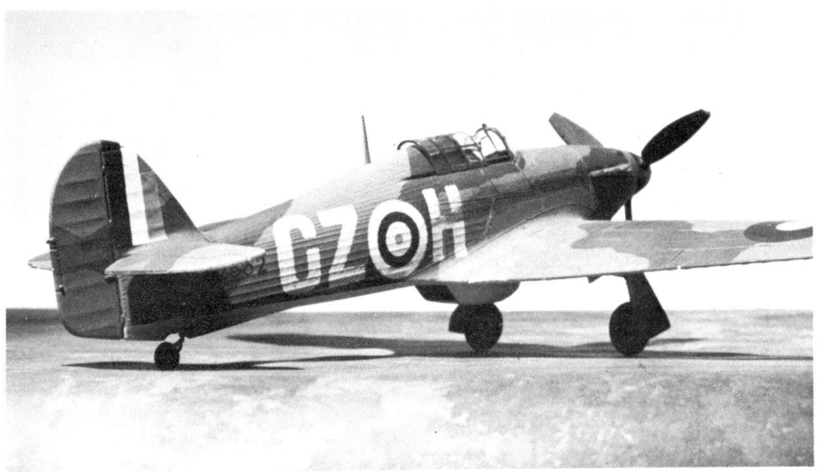

The use of a standard lens at an increased distance results in a better proportion between the tail and the rest of the model.

7〉

spective can be seen in fig. **1**, **2** and **3**. Notice how the "horizon", which in this case was the far edge of the board under the model, is reasonably sharp in fig. **1**, somewhat less sharp in fig. **2**, and distinctly woolly in fig. **3**. In all three cases the lens was stopped fully down. We should realize, however, that it is not the focal length of our lens which determines the perspective of a particular shot, but rather the point in space from which that particular shot is taken; the lens merely allows us to select a certain section of the scenery, and concentrate on our object. It is quite feasible for instance, to produce a picture such as fig. **3**, using the shorter focal length employed in fig. **1**. We would have to enlarge a very small portion of our negative to arrive at the same image size: on our negative the aircraft will be minute indeed.

In fig. **4** we can see the result of a lens working at its maximum opening; the depth of field is very shallow. Fig. **5** is the same shot with the lens closed down; the background now shows sufficient detail to create a feeling of reality. Finally, in fig. **6** we have the sometimes unpleasant side-effects of wide-angle photography: far too much emphasis is placed in this picture on the already large tail of the Hurricane. The remedy is to use a longer lens from a greater distance, as in fig. **7**.

Great care is called for when we are working with lenses of extremely short focal length; in a later chapter we will look at photographs taken with a special camera from a distance of 5cm, covering an angle of 100°.

CHAPTER

3 LIGHTING

Having discussed cameras, the next logical step is to examine our second most important set of tools: the lights. We have touched on this subject before, but now we shall investigate ways of using lights to the best advantage.

Our main objective is to duplicate, as closely as possible, average natural lighting conditions. When we know what Mother Nature does in her studio, we can do the same in ours. Under a wide, open sky, with a moderate cloud cover, diffused light travels in all directions. Ignoring the presence of the sun for a moment, we can say that this diffused light results in a fairly even illumination of the scenery. There are no shadows to speak of; deep crevices and similar openings appear darker, because little light will penetrate into them. Sharp shadows are completely absent. This sort of lighting does not really help in making details stand out or even become visible. A surface with a slight unevenness is likely to look perfectly smooth. A brick building will not show the individual bricks, as there are no little black shadows between them to make them stand out. Everything is rather flat.

In actual fact the light will never come evenly from all directions; our example is a purely theoretical one. The sun is always beating down on the clouds from somewhere above, and, depending on the thickness of the cloud layer, a spot will appear in the clouds which is much brighter than the rest. This area will act as a big, weak sun and throw our whole state of diffusion out of balance. Because it has a much larger diameter than the sun as it appears to us, the shadows it produces are so soft that we can hardly call them by that name. Still, the overall effect shows a vast improvement over the totally shadowless situation described earlier.

It is probably true to say that the heavier the cloud cover, the more even the lighting will be, although it will of course also be rather dark.

Now the sun comes back and takes control;

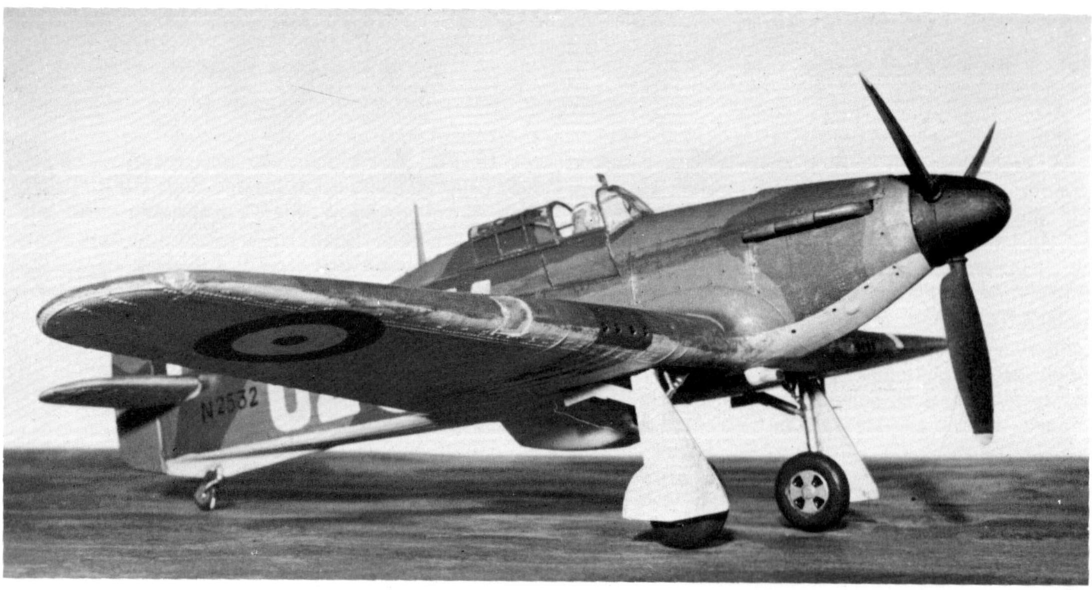

8

the diffused light remains, but strong directional light is added. Apart from raising the general level of illumination, this greatly enhances form and texture. The two photographs on these pages will illustrate this point.

Fig. **8** was taken with the light coming from a position fairly close to the camera lens. All the shadows are behind our object and serve no useful purpose. In fig. **9** the same light was located much higher. All the fine detail on the fuselage, virtually invisible in fig. **8**, suddenly appears. The fuselage itself, especially the nose-section, lacks any suggestion of roundness in fig. **8**; this is corrected by the improved lighting in fig. **9**. Another welcome benefit in this particular example is the disappearance of rather unwanted detail on the underside of the wing, just aft of the leading edge. Many plastic models, even some of the bigger ones, suffer from very pronounced rivet-lines. Despite the fact that an original aircraft was flush-rivetted we are all too often confronted with a model of it, sporting enormous rivet-heads. Our Hurricane was no exception, but this condition has been conveniently subdued in fig. **9**.

At this point we will have to define our terminology. If we place an object between a source of light and a screen, we will see that one side of our object is illuminated, while the other is dark; and also that the whole of the object throws a shadow on the screen. The dark side of the object is normally referred to as being in the 'shade', whereas the shadow on the screen, naturally enough, is known as the 'shadow'. In everyday language these terms are used fairly loosely, to which is added that some situations are very difficult to define anyway; it is hard to see which is which when shades merge into shadows, with possibly the shadow of an object nearby complicating things even further.

Generally speaking, however, we can say that a shade is always lighter in tone than a shadow; a fair amount of light reflects from the surface

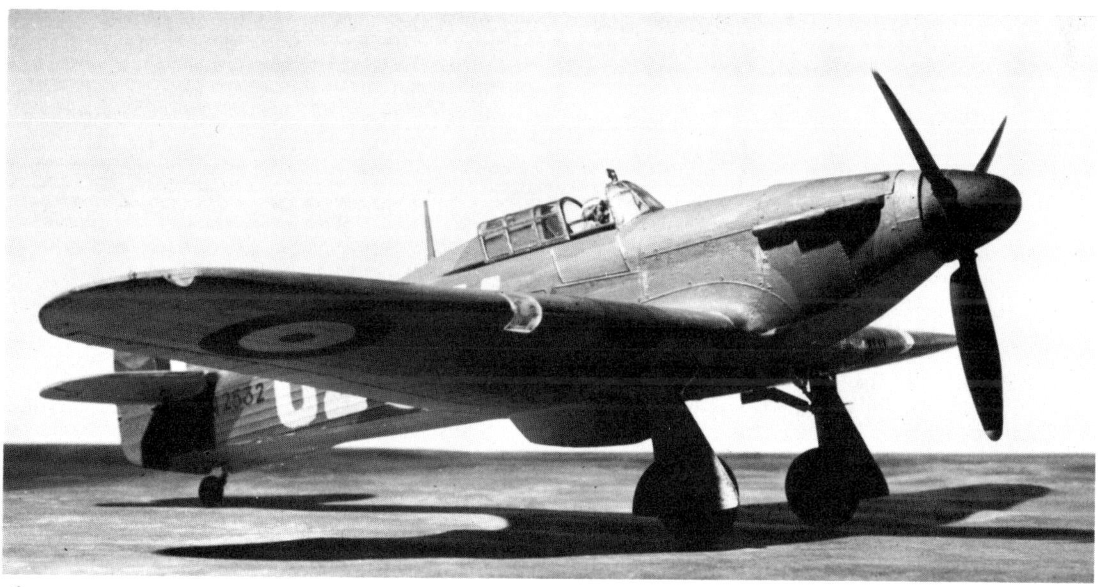

9

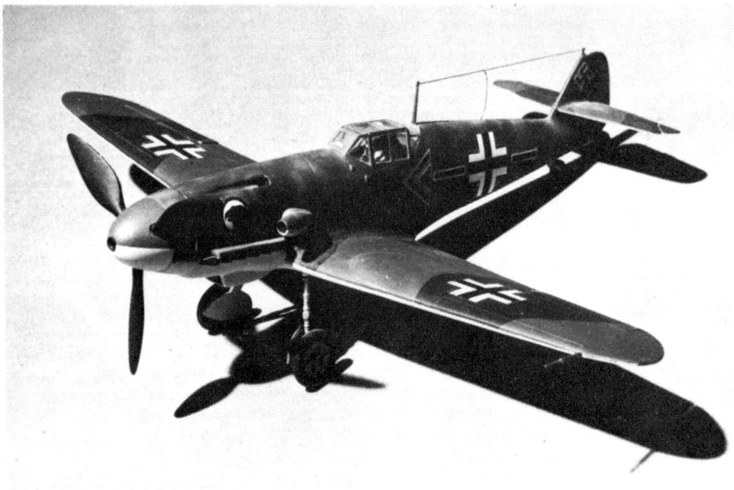

The shadow produced by a spotlight; this is the sort of shadow we find when the sun illuminates a scene: compare this with the shadows in figs. 11, 12 and 13.

10

onto which the shadow falls, back on the object itself. The level of illumination of this darkened side of our object depends of course on the amount of light reflected, in other words, on the tone and colour of the screen. If we choose to have a matt black surface, no light will be reflected at all and the shade will be as black as the night. A white screen reflects nearly all the light that falls on it, and we may in fact see very little difference between the bright part and what supposedly is the shade under those conditions. Two examples of these extremities, familiar to all of us, are on the one hand the half moon, where the darkened side is in effect completely invisible, and people in bright sunlight in the snow on the other; so much light is reflected by the snow, that the 'dark' side is almost as bright as the 'light' side. The attentive observer will have noticed, that just after the moon has been new, when only the narrowest slice of the bright side is coming into view again, all the rest of the moon, thought to be in darkness, is on the contrary clearly visible. Light reflected off the sunny side of the earth, is in turn reflected off the dark side of the moon, which in doing so becomes visible.

In general, however, the surfaces we are dealing with, will show an average degree of reflection. Only in those cases where our interference with the state of affairs is called for, will we use pure white reflectors.

In fig. **10** we see the kind of shadow produced by a spotlight; in this case a 500W spotlight with a front lens of 12-15 cm. We notice that the edges of this shadow are reasonably well defined. The sharpness of this outline is determined by both the size of our light-source and the distance between it and the object. It follows therefore, that with a large floodlight with a reflector of 35 cm or more, we will not be able to produce crisp shadows the same way as with our spotlight. The sun is in essence a very small point-source as far as we are concerned and the shadows it produces are characterised by this very crispness of outline. If we want to give our pictures that 'outdoor' look, we will have to pay special attention to this. The further away the spotlight, the sharper the shadow. It is even possible to produce soft shadows with a spotlight and such is the case if we place it too close to our model. This practice is a bad one, for three reasons: in the first place it is bad for our shadows, as just explained; secondly it would be very bad indeed for the model itself. Spotlights at close range are quite hot and we should not be too surprised to find our precious plastic model mutilated beyond recognition if left for any length of time in this fierce heat. Thirdly and perhaps equally important is the fact that the level of illumination by a spotlight increases by the square of the decrease of the distance; in other words, if we halve this

This shadow is too soft; notice how towards the edges it loses some of its intensity. The result is a very uneven tone of the shadow. This is the shadow produced by a single photoflood in a reflector of about 40 cm diameter.

11)

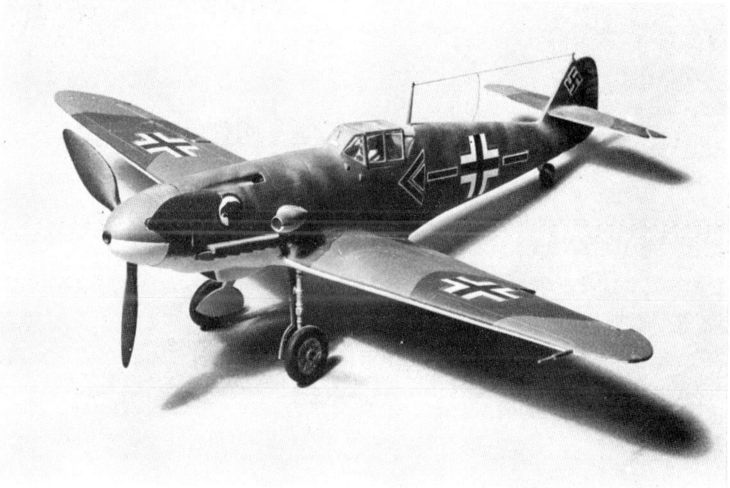

Two crossed shadows, each in turn killing the other. Where the two overlap (under the fuselage and wing) a very confusing form results, which draws more attention than the model itself. This arrangement is almost the worst possible - see fig. 13 for the ultimate!

12)

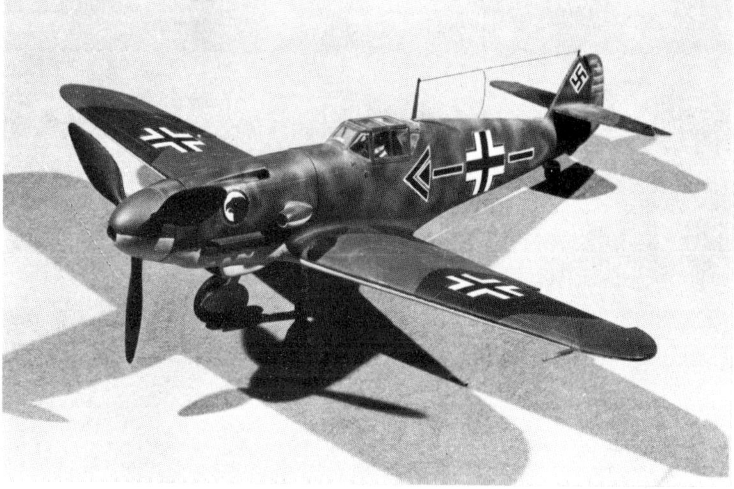

Brrr.!!!

13)

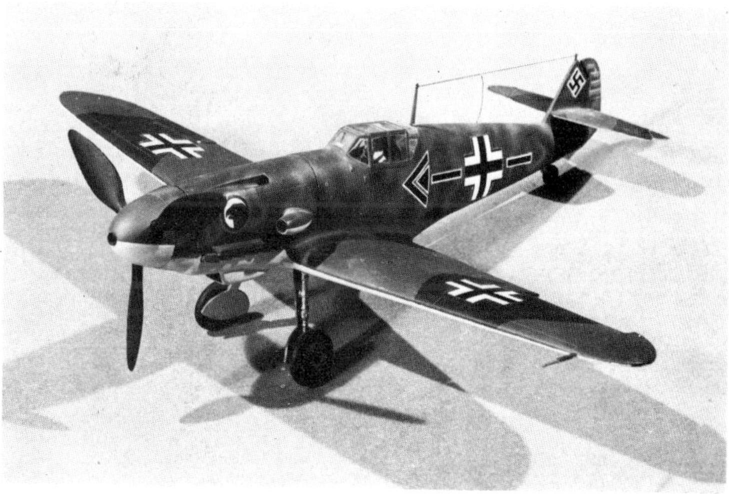

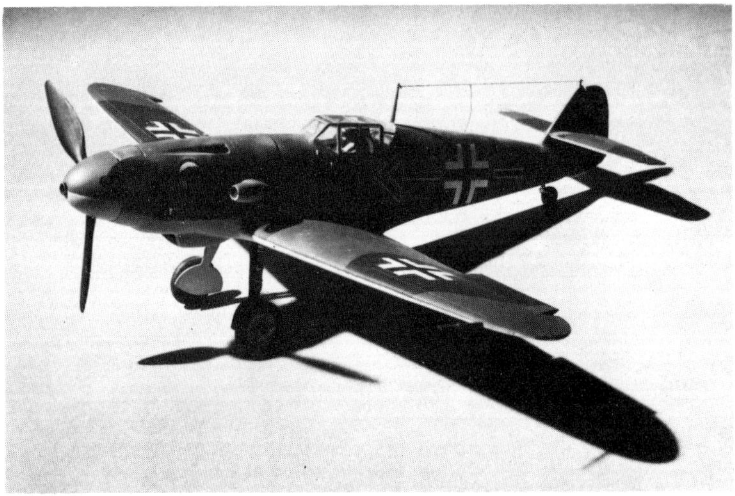

Spotlight only, no fill-in.

14

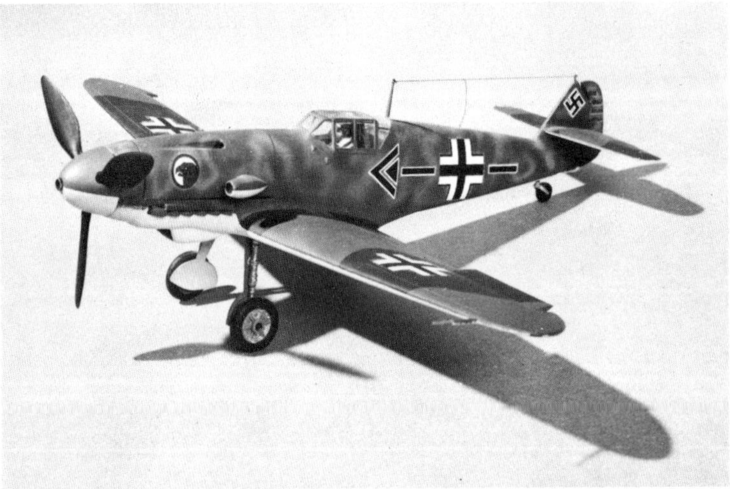

As above, but too much fill in.

15

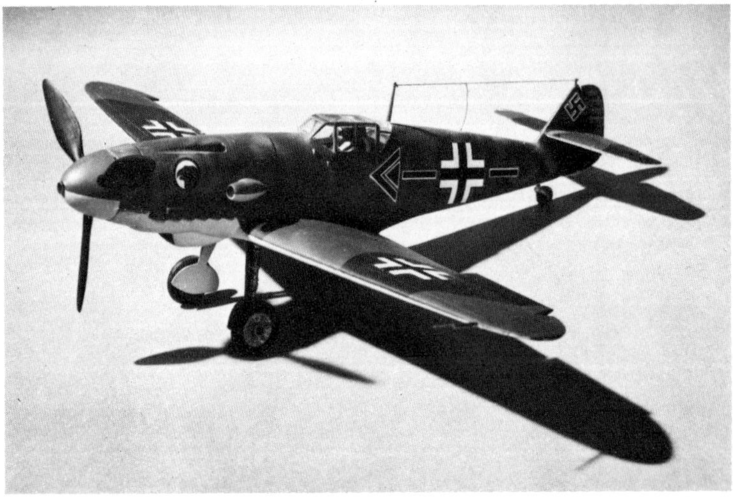

As above, properly balanced.

16

This is our first attempt to present a model in a more realistic way. Diagram A explains the details: for the sake of clarity the lighting arrangement is shown in its two components: a horizontal "cross-section" with the spotlight and a "plan-view" showing the illumination of the background. Limited space did not permit us to depict the spotlight at the distance from which we usually work it, which is approximately 150 cm. This applies to most of the following diagrams where a spotlight is indicated.

17

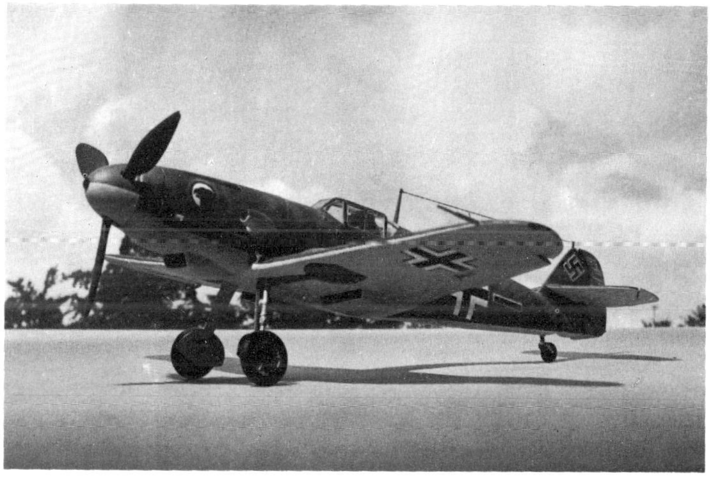

distance, we increase the intensity of the light four times. As a result, it becomes increasingly difficult to reach a satisfactory balance between mainlight and 'fill-in', as we call the diffused overall light.

In fig. **11** we used a large reflector-type floodlight. The resulting shadows could only be made by a sun trying to get through the clouds, and as such would still be acceptable. Fig. **12**, however, shows the thoughtless use of two spotlights, while fig. **13** is the ultimate in bad taste. Two spotlights, aided and abetted by a floodlight, create a chaotic maze of shadows, distracting from the actual picture. Notice how this profusion of light renders the model nearly flat; in fig. **11** there is still sufficient roundness in the model, while figs. **12** and **13** show a marked loss in this respect.

In fig. **14 - 16** we have raised the problem of the correct amount of fill-in. Before we realize it, we have too much, and the question is how to arrive at the proper level. Any direct light, even an open bulb of 100W would be too much, not to mention the crossed shadows this would leave us stranded with. The solution lies in the use of a white surface, reflecting some of the light from the spotlight. Placed vertically at the right hand side, out of sight of the camera, and positioned so that some light of the spotlight falls on it, this provides us with a very workable means of controlling the amount of fill-in. Fig. **14** shows us the set-up without reflector, while fig. **15** shows the effect of using a white sheet of cardboard of approximately 50cm square. The fill-in supplied by this was considered excessive and the area was reduced to about 1/6 of the original. The result is seen in fig. **16**.

From our point of view none of the examples **10 - 16** represents a good 'model' photograph. Whenever we take a shot of an object from some height, this object appears smaller than it should in the photograph that results. This applies to very large objects, such as buildings, which appear tall when viewed from the street below, and considerably less tall when seen from the roofs of adjoining buildings. It also applies to much smaller objects like furniture, even to the extent that when a familiar object such as a table is photographed from a normal viewing height, it appears unnaturally low to the ground. Of course, this is precisely the thing we want to avoid. Unfortunately, the only way to see how shadows are formed, is to look at them from some height.

The low-level shot in fig. **17** is much closer to being a good model photograph. Here a cloud background has been introduced; you will remember that it was stressed how important clouds are in our attempts to create atmosphere and depth. We are not ruling out pictures taken

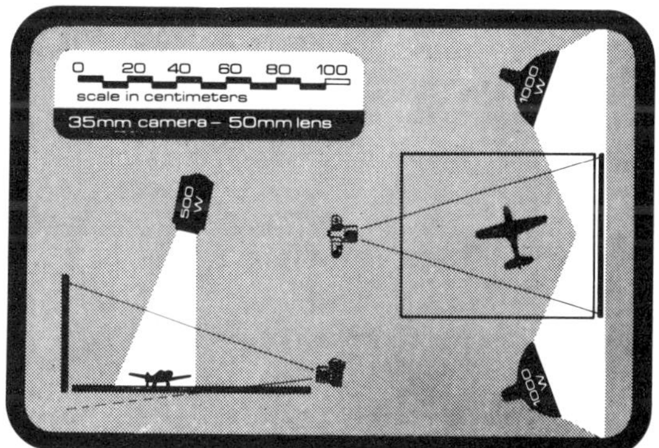

A

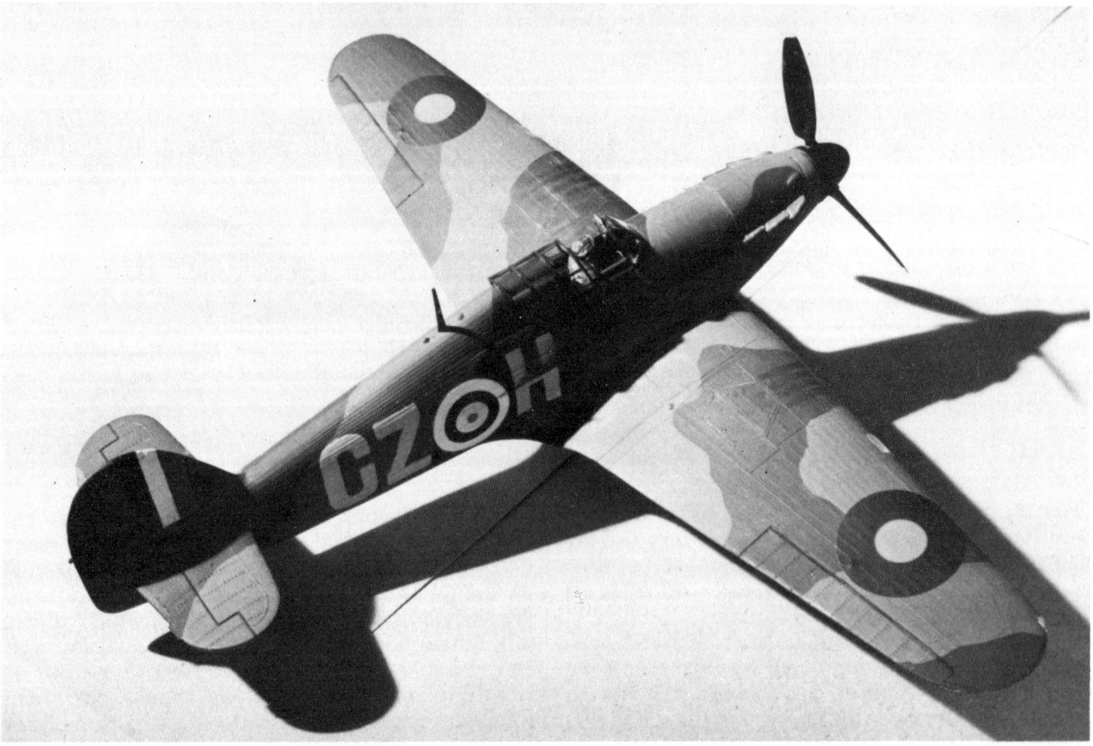

〈18

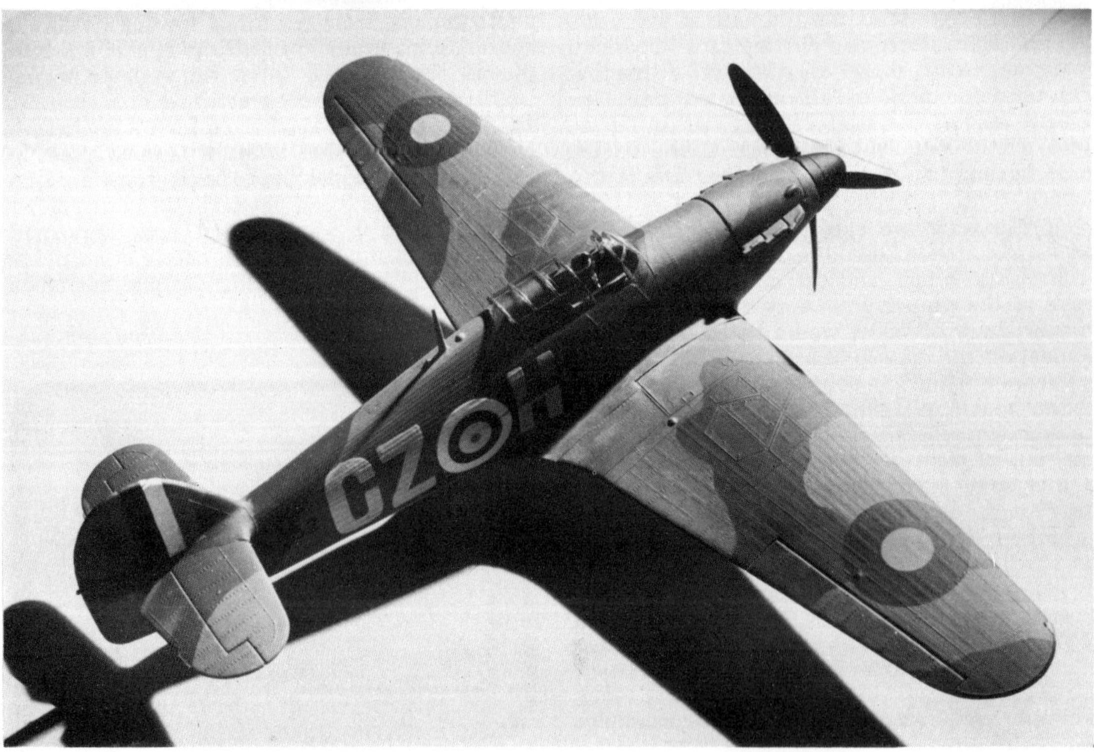

〈1

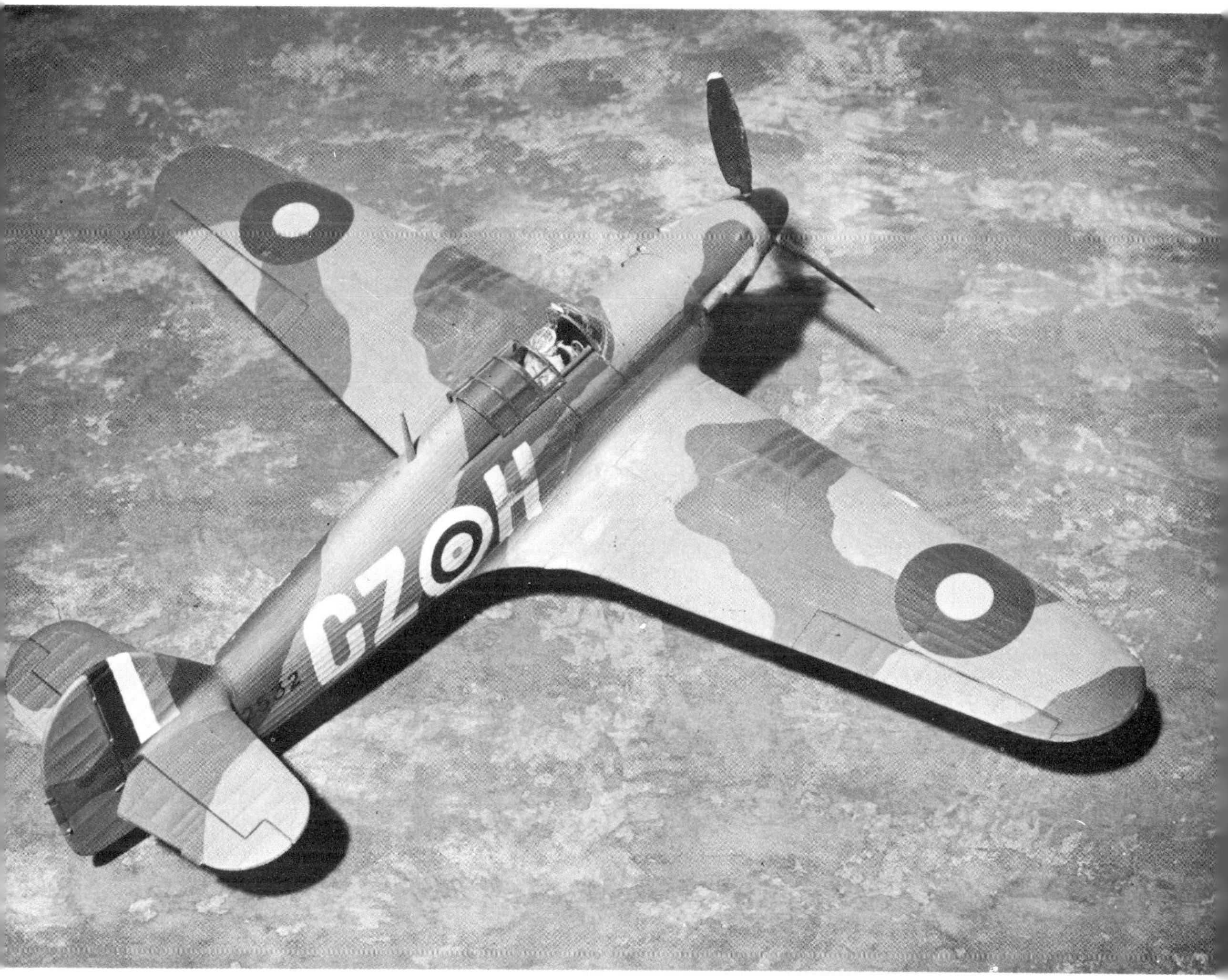

from some height; they tend to show us more of the model than the very low-level ones ever could, revealing otherwise hidden features. Advertisements frequently use this approach, although, almost without exception, they suffer from either very soft shadows or the chaotic multitude. Perhaps these photographs do not pretend to be any more than model-photographs, but, in not doing so, they seem somehow to defy their purpose.

In fig. **18** we have tried to find out how a strong, dominating shadow can destroy a picture. The wing and its shadow virtually coincide, thus confusing us, while the fuselage and its shadow, for their part, form a strong pattern right across the page, which, in this photograph at least, does not add much to the visual appeal of the composition. We moved our mainlight to the right hand side in such a way that the model and its shadows were no longer interfering with each other, as in fig. **19** We will always encounter this situation, if we insist on taking our photographs from a high view-point; a fully satisfactory answer is not easily found and we will therefore consider the problem arising from this approach as another argument against.

In fig. **20** we placed our model on a background we were to use in a later photograph with a much larger model; the texture suggests an irregular grass surface. Notice how the model does not manage to 'come out of' the background; if it were not for the fairly strong shadows we could hardly see it. We must admit that this, of course,

21

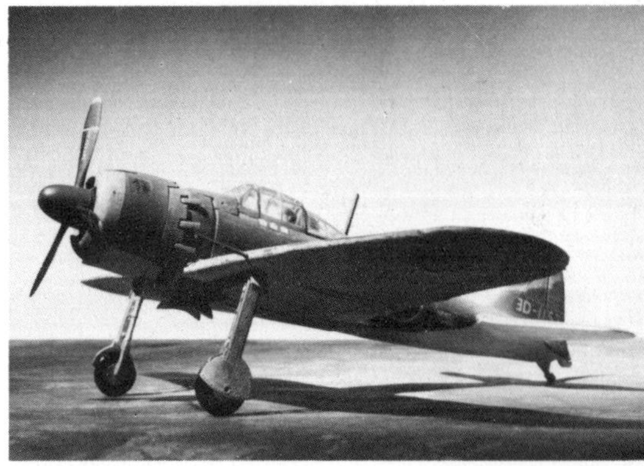

is the very essence of camouflage, and it does prove a point, but it does not make a pleasing picture. In figs. **18** and **19** we used a background of cardboard tiles, tentatively smudged to resemble a concrete surface. As it turned out, however, they were far too light in tone, which resulted in relative over-exposure with consequent loss of all detail. It requires a fair amount of practice to know exactly which model looks best on what background, but we will do well to start with one that is not too light, bearing in mind that photographic film can reproduce only a certain contrast range — if we exceed this, either the darker part (the model) or the lighter part (the background) will suffer. Judging contrast with the unaided and un-trained eye can be very deceptive indeed; our eyes are equipped with a fully automatic diaphragm and we see a very bright area, for example, darker than it really is, because as soon as we look at it, the iris closes. The opposite happens if we concentrate on a darker area.

Although the total field of view of our eyes is fairly wide, we can concentrate on only a very small area. This is because in the centre of the retina the nerve-ends are much more numerous, and so our vision in this region is much better. Our eyes are restlessly scanning the entire scene, the iris opening and closing as we look at darker and brighter parts respectively. Inevitably we will get the impression that we have arranged everything pretty well and we will feel quite pleased with ourselves — until we begin to print our film and we find that we have been tricked. To avoid frustrations of this kind, we should keep our contrast fairly low by means of adequate fill-in, and later of course, with some practice, we will know exactly what to do.

A good example of the sort of photograph where an excessive contrast is likely to occur, if not actually called for, is a shot taken at night. A distinctive feature will be the total absence of 'fill-in' light, while the main illumination will, in general, come from a small but strong spotlight, some distance away.

In fig. **22** we started with a standard setting; spotlight on the model, two floodlights on either side of the background. We turned off the lights illuminating the plain background, and there we had our night shot! Or did we? Upon reflection we realised that on an airfield any lights would be located fairly close to the ground; certainly if our model were to be put at some distance from this light, as would be the case if the aircraft was somewhere in the middle of the field, the effective angle of illumination would be very shallow

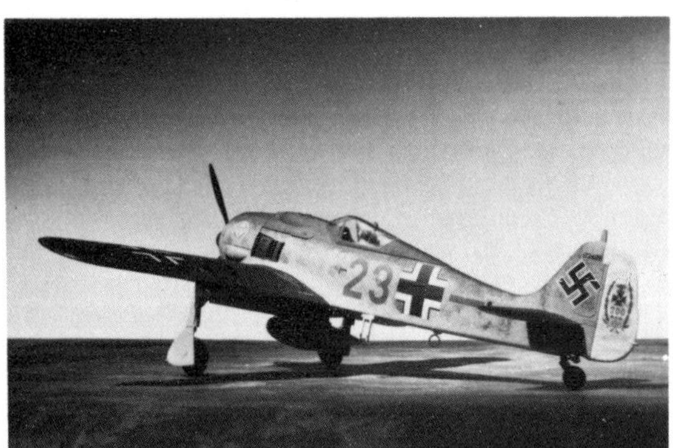

22

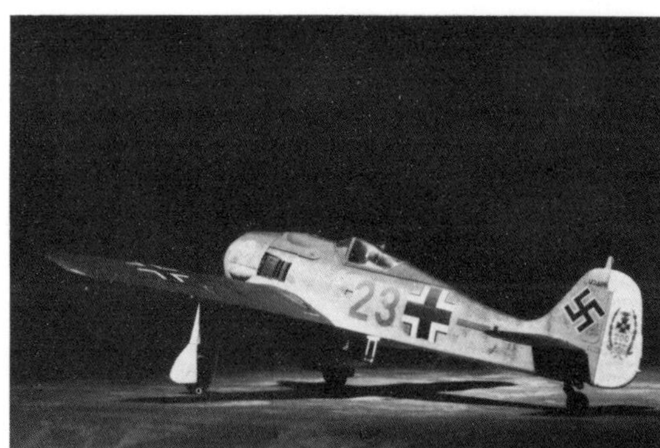

23

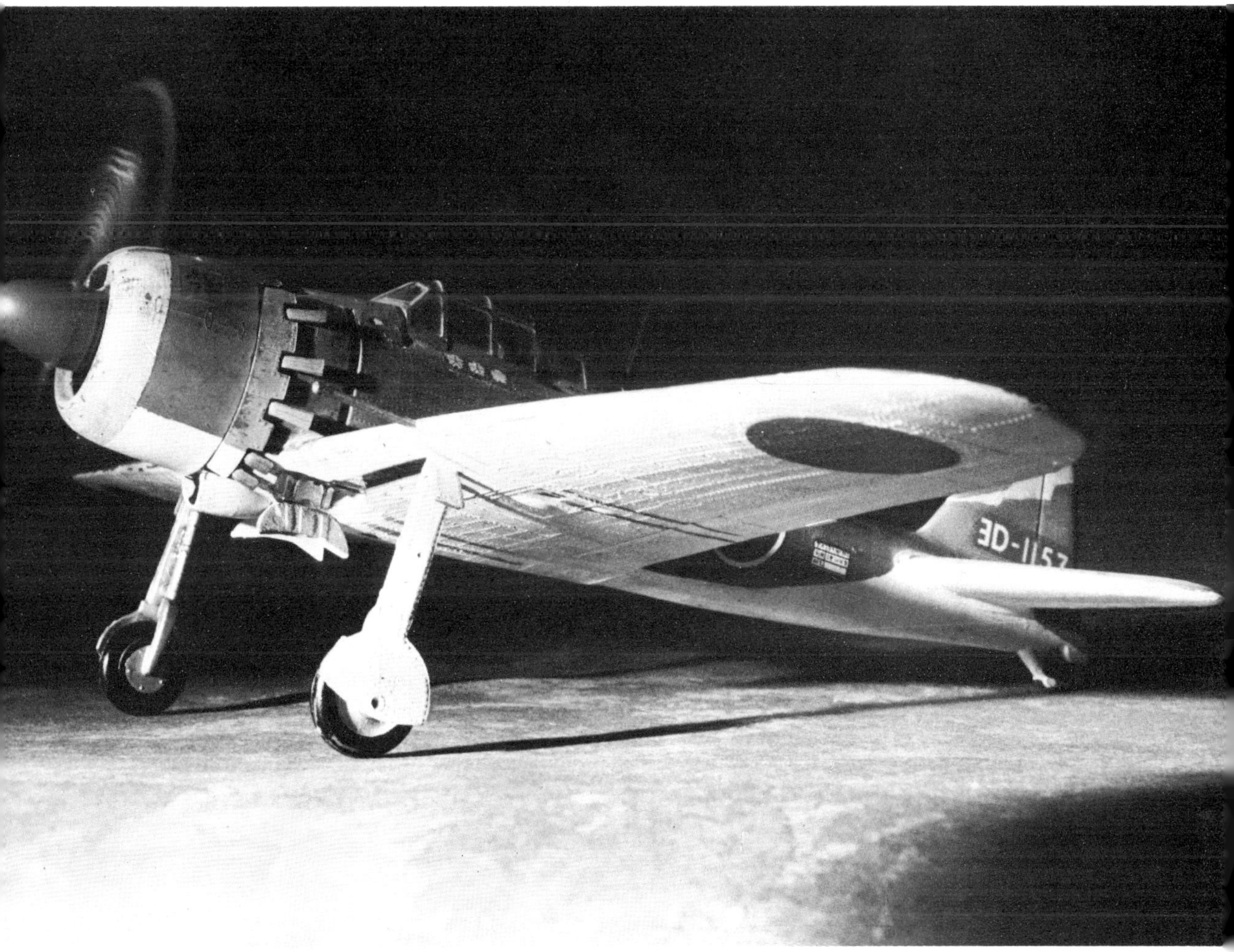

24

indeed, and would definitely not come from almost directly overhead, as in fig. 23.

Consequently we lowered our spotlight to nearly horizontal and tried it again. There is plenty of evidence of a high contrast in the resulting print: notice how there isn't much detail left in leading edges and wheel covers. All this is acceptable, however, because under unfavourable circumstances as these, one does not expect a top quality photograph in the sense that highlights and shadows are fully detailed. In fig. 21 we can see how things were before the lights went out.

Briefly then, the lighting conditions that prevail during the night are: total darkness, broken by usually one strong light source, located behind the camera or to one side of it — never coming directly towards us! It is not uncommon to find two or even more such spotlights illuminating the scene. If we chose to reproduce a situation as this, the use of crossed spotlights, so strongly criticised earlier, is fully justified.

The relatively low level of illumination forces us to make fairly long exposures. As we will see, a revving propeller requires very little time to become quite invisible. In fig. 24 we blew on the prop to make it turn; we notice that whatever remained visible appears to be blurred and almost double exposed. This was due to this particular propeller not running true, each blade travelling as it were its own way. Many things can go wrong with moving parts and in the next chapter we shall see some of the more obvious ones; we shall discuss ways to make stubborn propellers behave as they never behaved before.

CHAPTER

4 MOVING PARTS

The most important moving part on any aircraft is undoubtedly the propeller, assuming always that it has one. It is difficult to take a photograph of an aeroplane without putting some degree of emphasis on this vital part, and we can conveniently divide the possibilities here into two groups; those with the propeller stationary and those with it revolving.

One of the golden, even if unwritten, rules of photography, where pictures of people are concerned, is never to show a person in such a way, that he or she appears to have lost an arm or leg. The difference between a photograph that passes this test and one that fails it, is very subtle. You need to show only a very small bit of shoe, knee or elbow to make the person in question complete. This very same rule applies to propellers of aircraft.

Look closely at fig. **25** and the more you study it, the more you will feel the urge to turn that spinner around a bit to see if the third and up till now invisible blade is there. Fig. **26** shows some improvement; the three blades are all there, but the nearest one is not really well enough defined against the dark background of the cowling. Fig. **27**, the last one in this short series of prop-

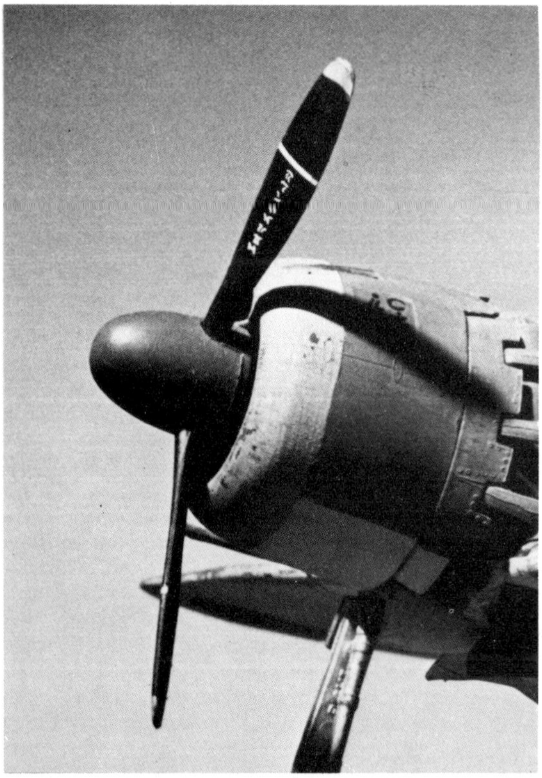

25

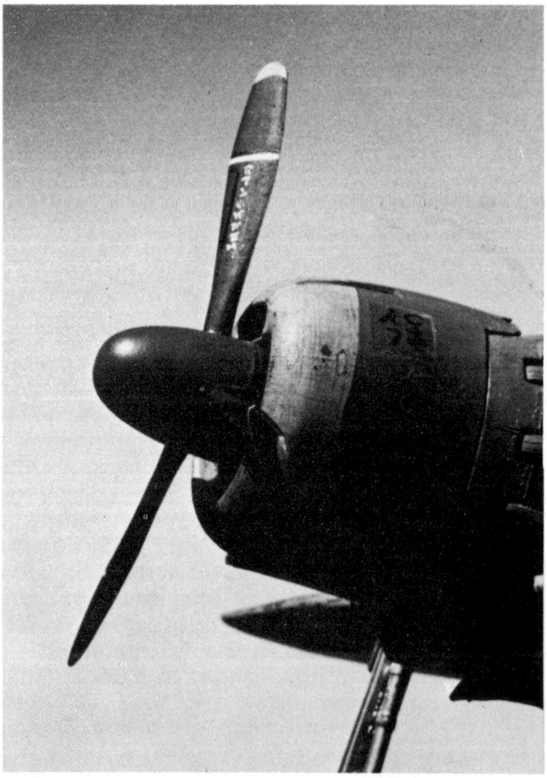

26

ellers at rest, is the final solution. It is quite possible of course (and I must admit that I am not enough informed on this subject) that every airforce has its regulations regarding the position of a propeller when it is not being used; in fig. **27** it seems to offer the least risk of people running into it while the aircraft is being serviced.

Fig. **28**, need we mention it, shows our prop revving. With the engine idling, which is the most likely way we will find our aircraft, the propeller is doing about 800 to 1000 rpm; this is the equivalent of roughly 13 to 16 revolutions per second. If we take our picture at 1/1000 of a second, then the prop gets the chance to move only 1/1000 of about 13 revs, which is approximately 5^{0} of the full circle. This makes it almost seem to be at a standstill; only a very slight blur will appear at the propeller tip. At a slower shutter speed we will get proportionately more movement and fig. **29** is roughly the equivalent of what happens at 1/500 of a second, while fig. **30**, with nearly twice the amount of movement, shows the situation at 1/250 of a second. At slower speeds still, the propeller will disappear altogether.

The problem we have on our hands now, however, is that in our studio we will never have

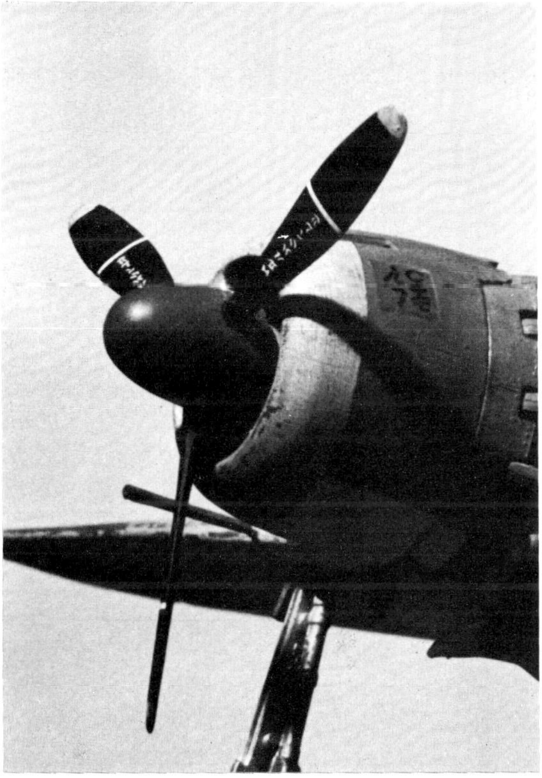

27

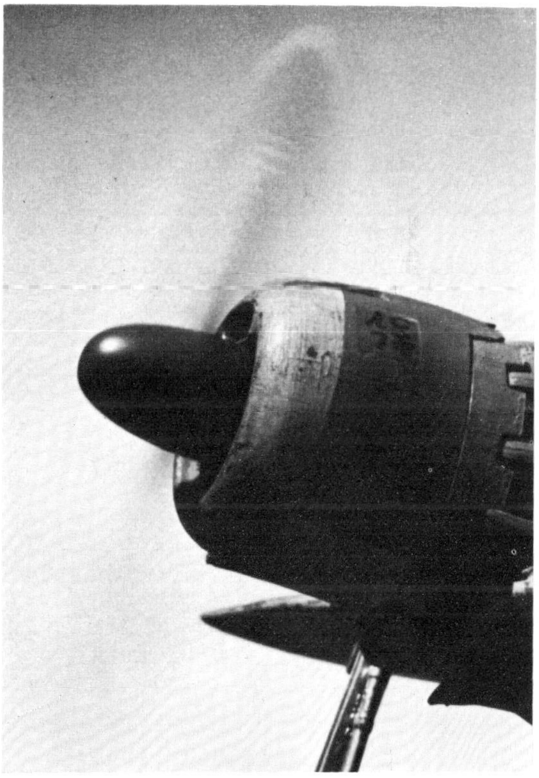

28

the amount of light available that would allow us to work with these short exposure times, apart from the fact that we had just decided to work only with our lens closed as far as possible; we are of course using fairly slow film to keep the grain at bay or maybe we even have colour reversal film in our camera, which is slower still. None of these factors are of any help at all if we are trying to give the impression of a short exposure time having been used. The shutter speed necessary with even reasonably strong lights will never be shorter than about ½ second. The answer is therefore to get our propellers to move very slowly. In fig. **29** and **30** we did expose for only a short period of time and the lens had to be opened wide; result: no depth of field!

A lot depends on how we have assembled our model; also the size of it throws in a lot of weight, literally! A large airscrew will build up so much momentum that it will go on revolving for a short while. The very small ones, on the other hand, even though they pick up speed fast, will quickly lose it again. The old flick with the finger is not always the answer because the jerk of it may upset the model and leave it shuddering. A little very thin lubricating oil on the shaft will

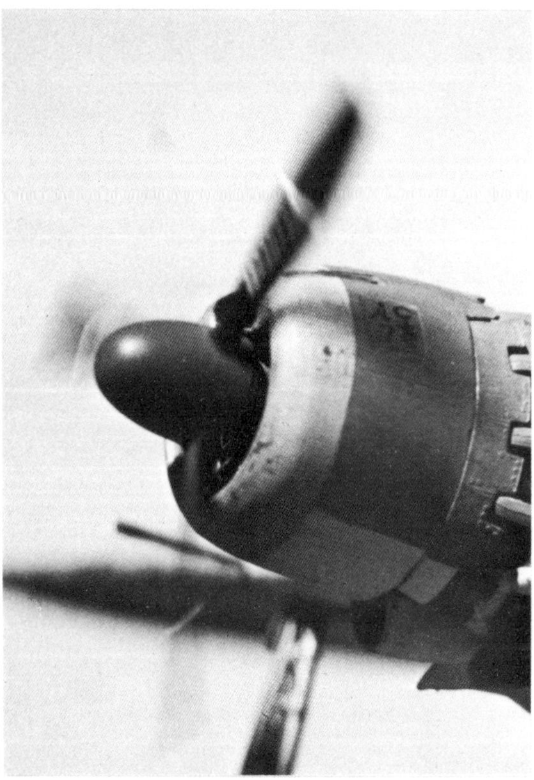

29

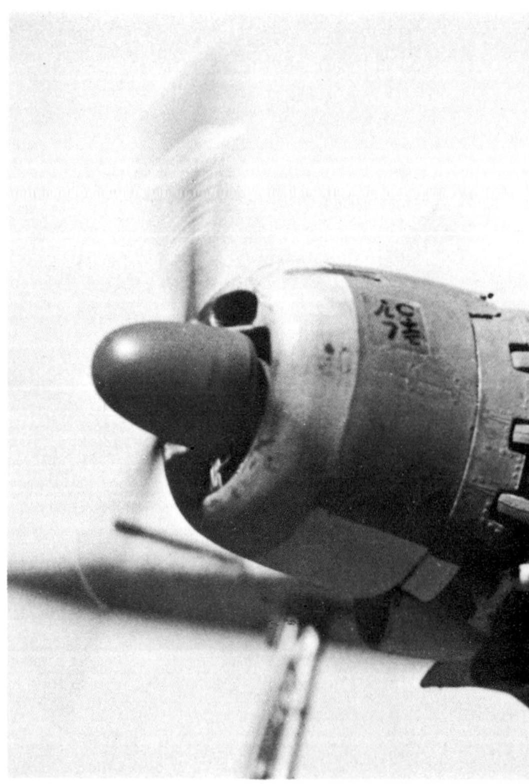

30

overcome most of these problems, and with some practice we will quickly teach ourselves how to get things just right.

It will, however, not always be possible to arrive at the amount of propeller movement shown in fig. **29** and **30**, nor is this absolutely necessary. More often than not we will have to be satisfied with the state of affairs as depicted in fig. **28**, which, after all, is quite acceptable.

In the remaining three photographs we can see what happens when, for instance, our timing is a bit off: Fig. **31** is the prop that stopped before the shutter closed, while fig. **32** and **33** are vary-

31

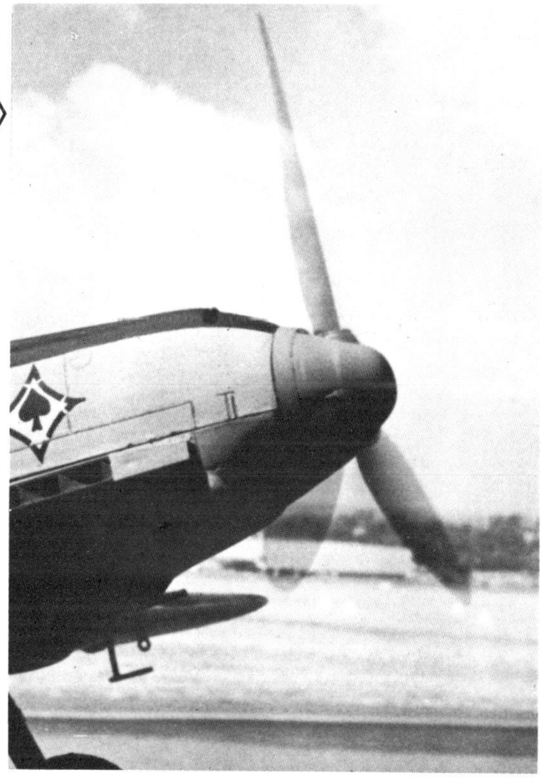

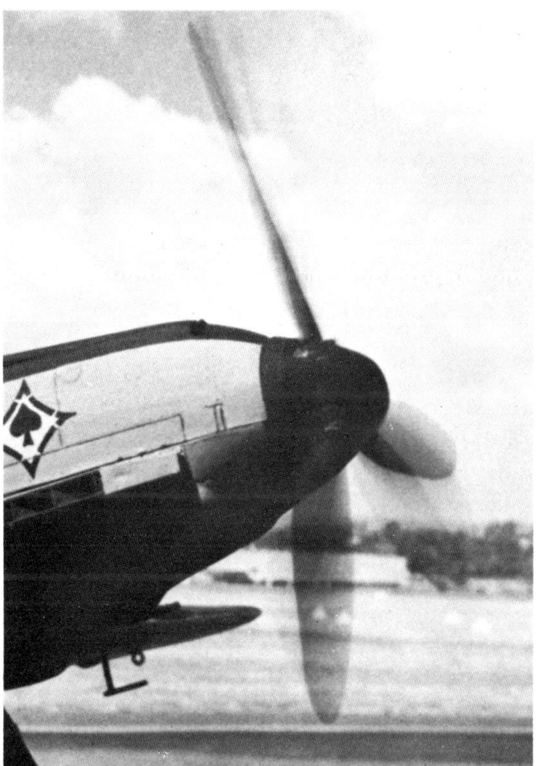

32

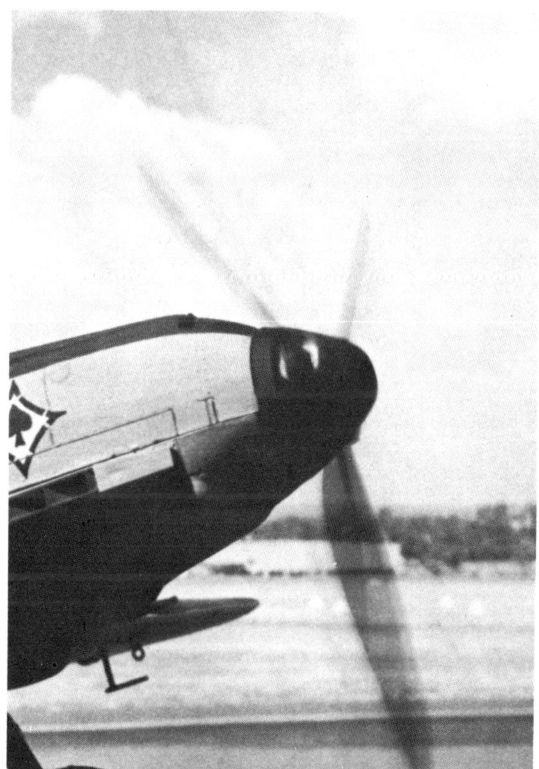

33

ing stages of hesitatingly revolving propellers. This is most likely to happen when we decide on the blow-method: we cannot be expected to give out a strong, continuous airstream for the length of time that we need it, which may be as much as six or eight seconds. Most of us will have to gasp for some air between short bursts, and if our prop is not of the co-operative kind, this is the result.

On the other hand, it may be inadvisable to blow on the aircraft; such was the case when we tried to photograph the model in fig. **36**: it simply flew off the set. There are ways to overcome this kind of handicap, which, we must admit, took us by surprise. The simplest method involves the use of a long steel rod, preferably gauge 20 or 22, matt-painted in a tone matching the background, as illustrated in fig. **35**.

The principle is to set up an even revolving movement with the rod; make sure the hand hold-it does not appear in the picture! Beware of any uninvited shadows. In the excitement of the moment it is surprisingly easy to overlook those little details, which turn into big spoilers, if allowed to go unchecked. If we aim to turn the prop round once every second, then this will make it fairly easy to count off the seconds of our exposure time. Doing this, you will soon discover that you could do with another pair of hands on many an occasion, especially when trying to turn a little prop round with one hand sometimes balancing a tripod which has to lean out at an awkward angle. The secret of success lies in not allowing the rod to come to a stop, preferably making it go a little faster around the top and the bottom of its circle; any hesitation at these points will immediately become visible. The thinner the rod we use, the better, provided we can still adequately control the prop with it. The situation in fig. **34** makes it clear that some action on our part is called for; an aircraft apparently flying normally, but with an airscrew, doing nothing, just sitting there, leaves something to be desired. Fig. **35** shows our little rod coming to the rescue, while fig. **36** is the final result. It could be argued here that the rod we used was too dark. Just in front of the propeller, bleeding out of the picture, is a darker area, barely noticeable, but nevertheless there. Some of the light on its way to the camera from the sky direct-behind, has been absorbed by the rod; a lighter and thinner one would undoubtedly have absorbed less. This has to be tried out; in the extreme case of a solid black background it would not matter what gauge black rod we used, whereas against a delicate grey we would have to be very careful indeed. The principles outlined here can be applied to many other fields of scale modelling.

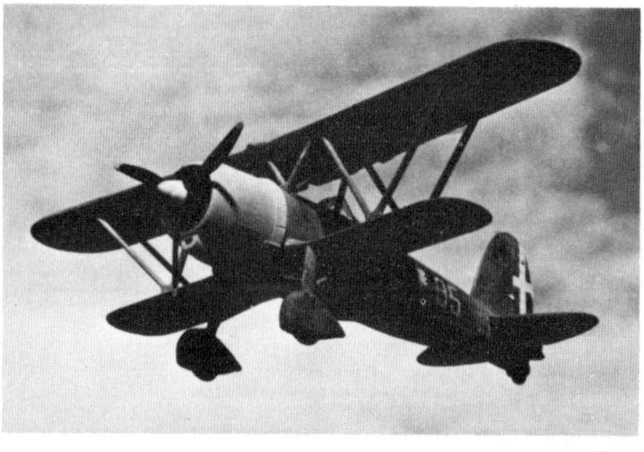

34

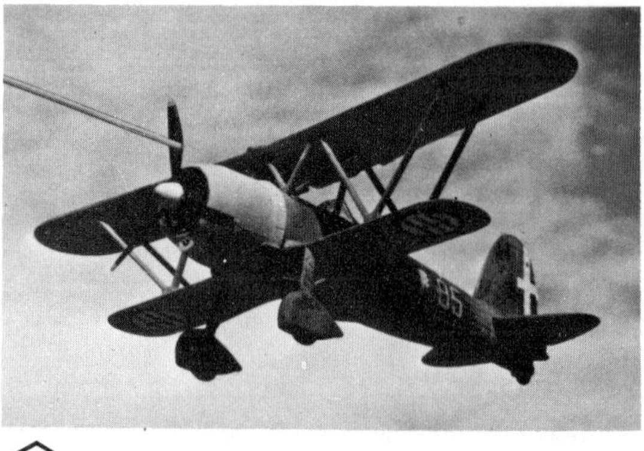

35

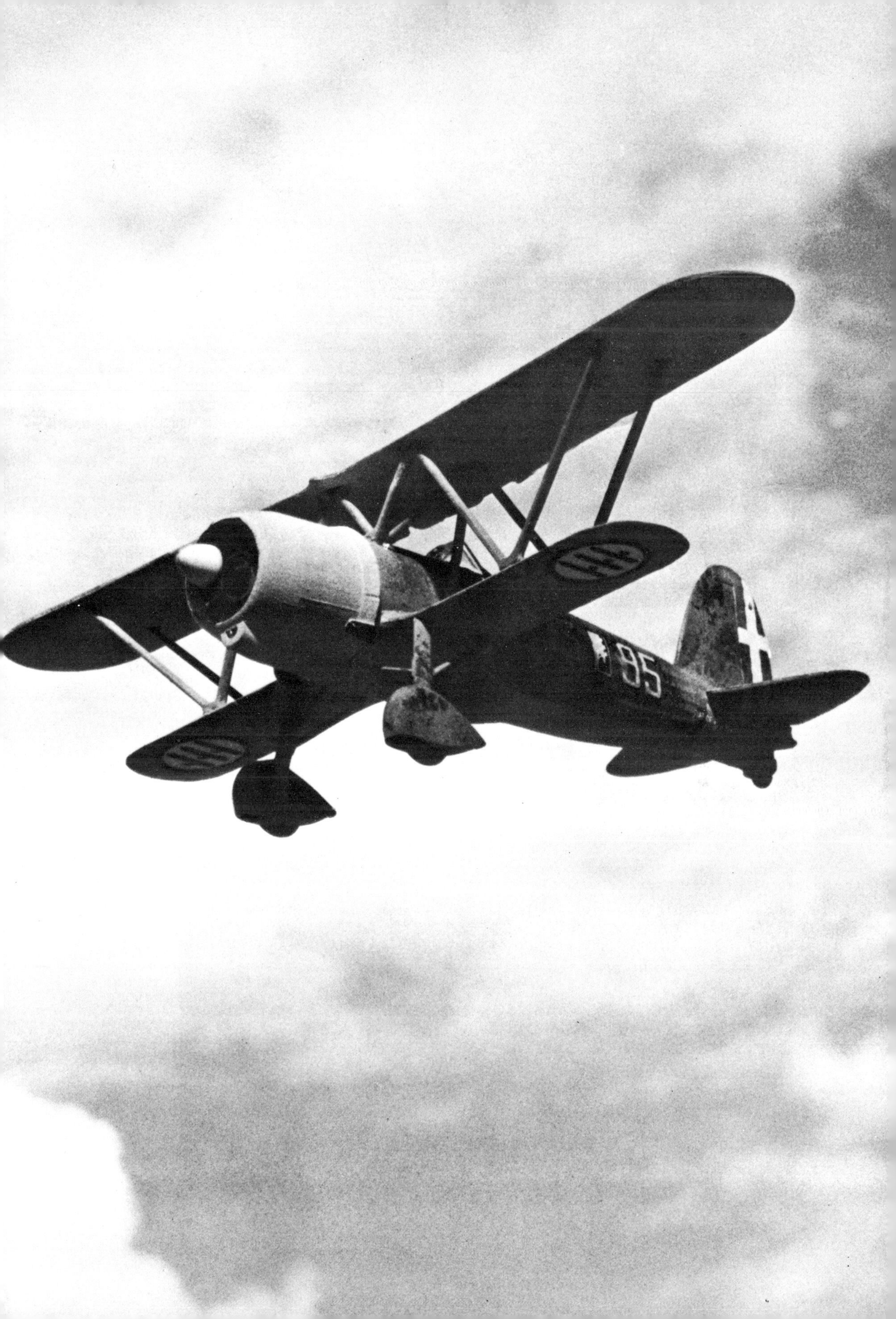
95

CHAPTER

5 FILTERS

This subject could well be considered as belonging in a book about basic photography: we will deal with it briefly however.

The nature of the camouflage of many aircraft is such that it tends to make them inconspicuous against certain backgrounds. This doubtless virtue during hostilities leads to less desirable effects in our pictures.

The colours used in the great majority of camouflage patterns are fairly similar in grey-value, which means that when these colours are photographed on panchromatic film, they appear as almost the same tone of grey. What this does to the actual pattern can easily be seen.

This book is not the place to treat colour theory exhaustively; be it enough to state that a colour filter lets only light of its own colour pass through. In other words, we see a red filter as red because only red light comes through it. All other colours are stopped, especially blue and green. This is fairly simple.

Now let us see what this means to us in practice and how we can make use of this property to restore those seemingly lost tonal differences and so improve the quality of our photographs.

In figs. **37-40** we have a Bf 109 G, painted in the typical colours of its day. All flying surfaces are in two shades of green — dark green and very dark green. The fuselage sides and fin have a mottled, soft-sprayed pattern, again in blue-green-grey colours. In a situation such as this, where all our colours fall more or less in the same group, we can do pitifully little with our filters to alter the distinction between the one colour and the next. No matter what filter we try, it has an equal effect on all the colours, making them all lighter or all darker. The final impression is the same in all cases.

By way of contrast we did the same with a Macchi Folgore, the two upper-surface colours of which are very close in grey-value, but fall in two directly opposite colour groups. This provided an excellent example of a pattern disappearing under certain conditions.

We can influence any colour in two ways: we can either lighten it by using a filter of its own colour, or we can darken it by using a filter of the opposite colour. For those unfamiliar with these terms, we will spend a few words on this subject. When the colours of the spectrum are placed in a circle, any given colour will find itself directly

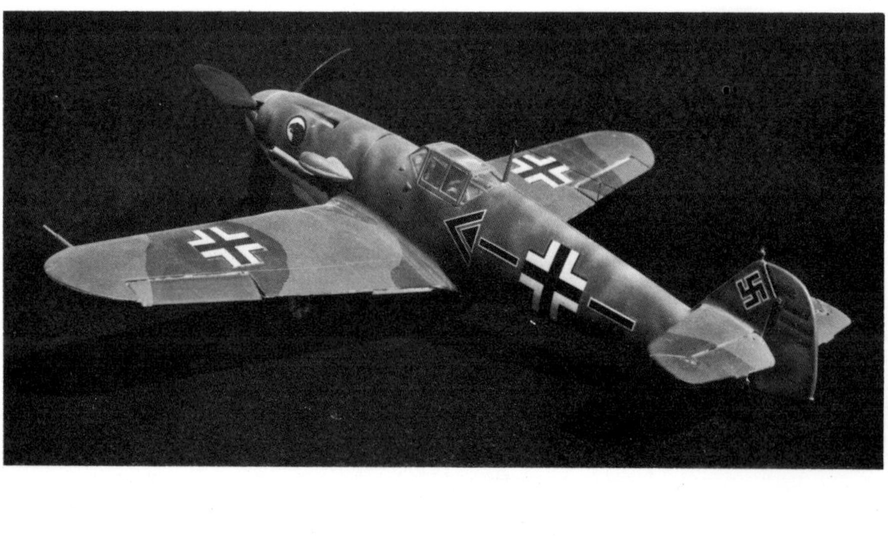

37

This is how dark green and black green look under direct sunlight.

38

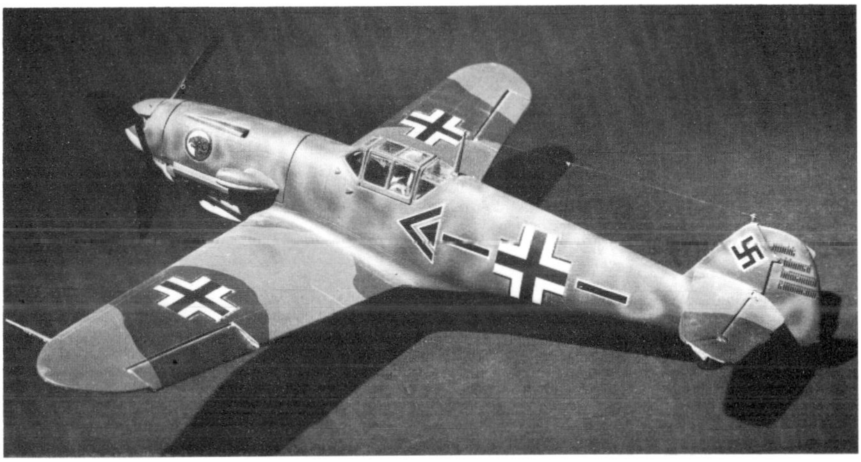

In this and the following two pictures we see a slight increase in contrast due to the higher percentage of red light present in tungsten light.

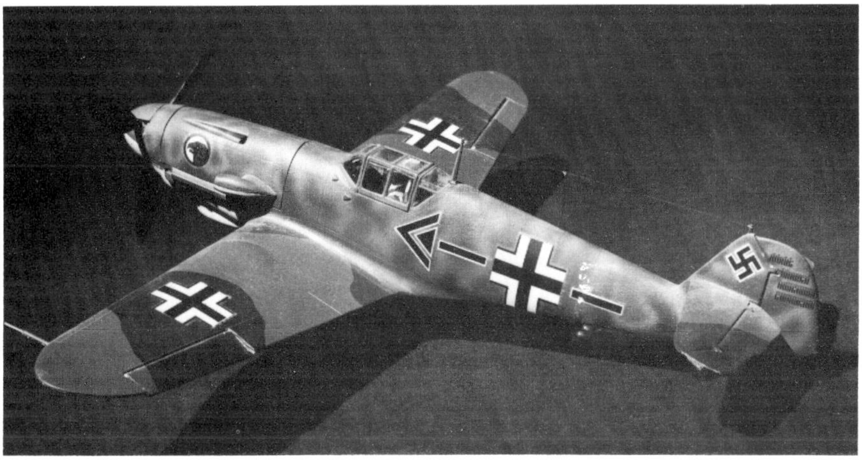

39

A yellow filter does not alter the relation between these colours much.

40

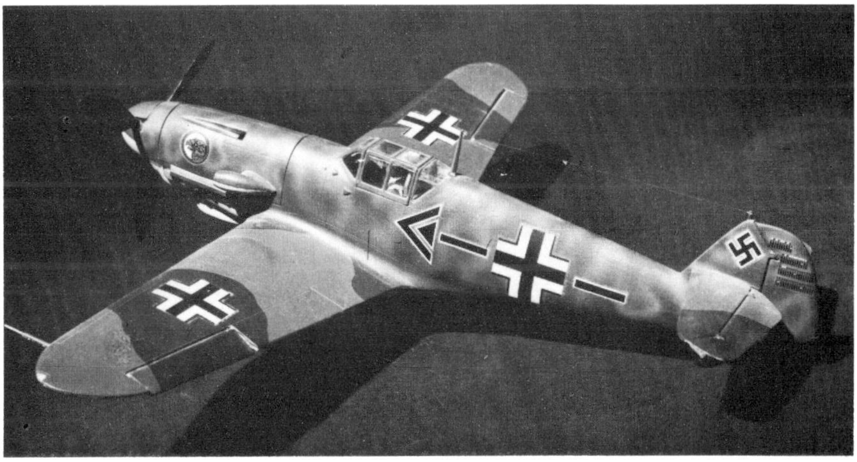

Because of the high percentage of red light, which in itself effects a certain degree of red-filtering, a red filter has no noticeable effect.

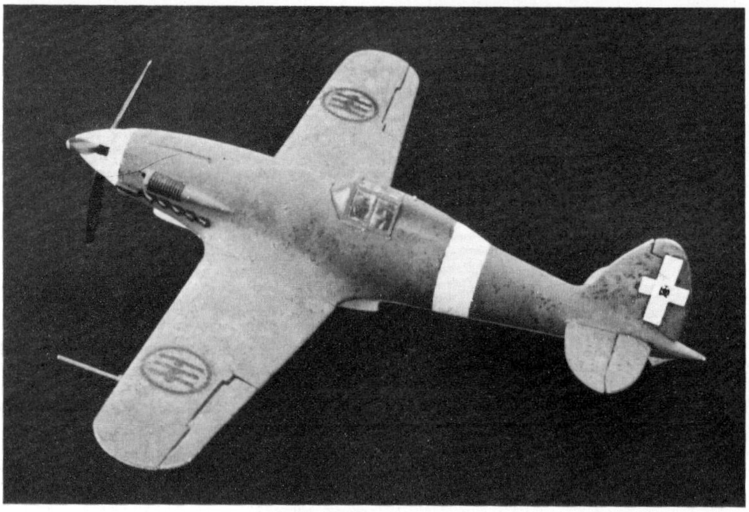

41

In this case diffused sunlight almost obliterated the otherwise very clear distinction between the two colours used on this model.

opposite another colour, literally on the other side of the circle. In this way red is the opposite of green, blue the opposite of yellow, etc. We realize that the matter really is a bit more complicated than this simple explanation would suggest, but for the purpose of playing around with a few filters, we do not have to go into any great detail.

Better than a thousand words are the eleven pictures with which we hope to make ourselves clear. As we did with the Messerschmitt, we started the experiment by showing how the colours are rendered in daylight. Diffused skylight, containing a higher percentage of blue light than direct sunlight, all but obliterated the pattern (fig. **41**). Brought into the sun, which contains more red and yellow, we see a slight improvement (fig. **42**). Figs. **43-45**, all taken in the studio with artificial light, show an increasing darkening of the green, due to stronger red filtering, partly because tungsten light contains a high percentage of red. In fig. **44** we used a light blue filter, which converts artificial light to average daylight, and the effect is, if anything, a slight deterioration of the distinction between the two colours. Finally, in fig. **45**, we used a red filter; the results obtained with a filter as strong as this are somewhat diminished by the fact that artificial light was used in the first place. The same filter, used in daylight, has a much greater effect.

Then, on the other hand, we may want to suppress a certain colour, in which case we simply apply this theory in reverse. If, for whatever

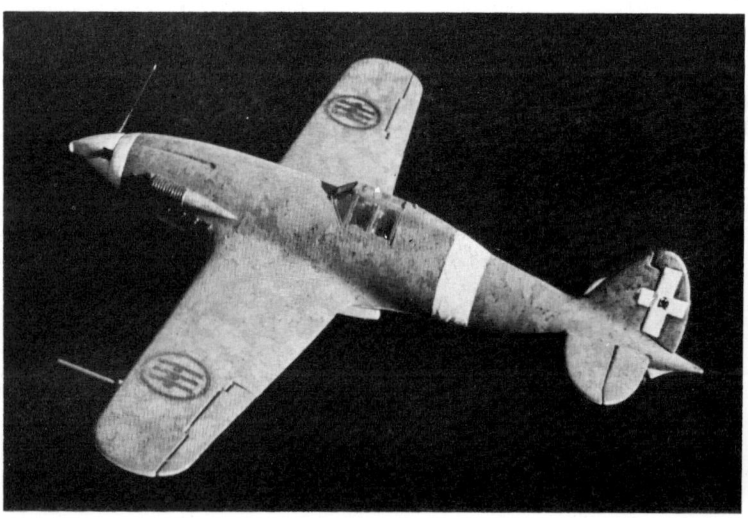

42

Direct sunlight contains less blue light than light coming from a blue sky, as in fig. 41; therefore the green patches appear slightly darker than they did under diffused skylight. Notice a slight improvement in the general rendition of the colours.

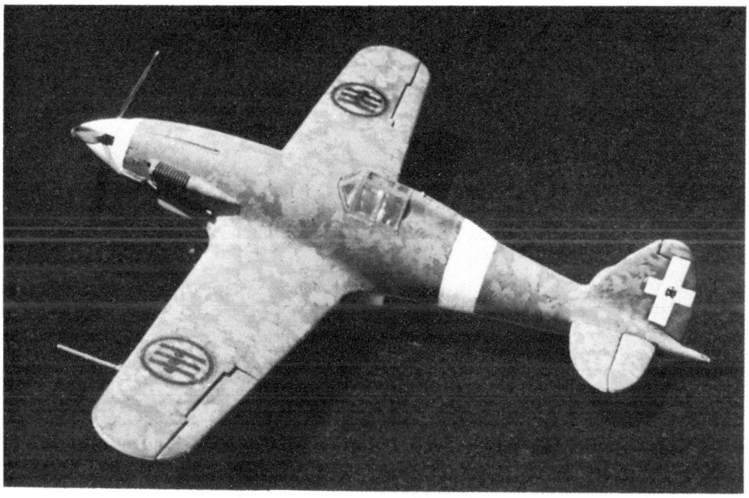

43

Tungsten light, containing a higher percentage of red light, darkens the green and the pattern becomes clearly visible.

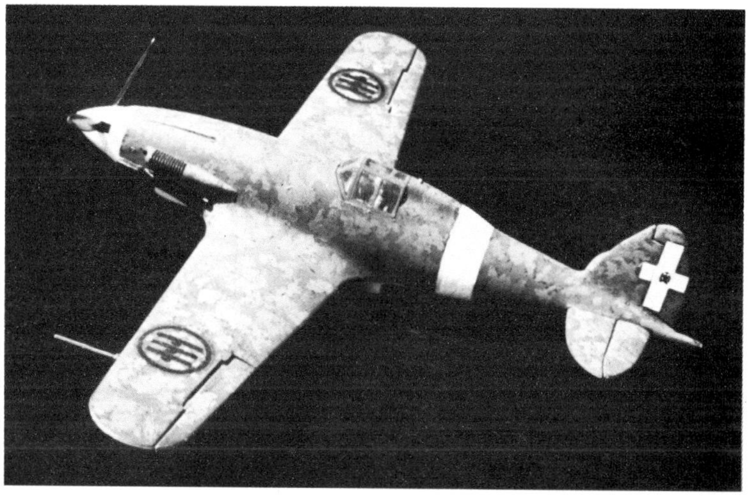

44

A light blue filter, used to convert tungsten light to average daylight, has little effect; if anything, the contrast has deteriorated a little.

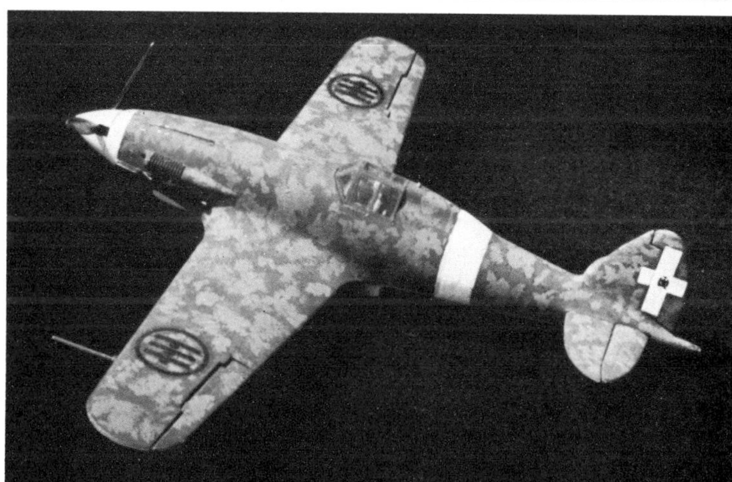

45

Because a red filter has a relatively strong effect on colours such as blue and green, we see a marked improvement in the pattern.

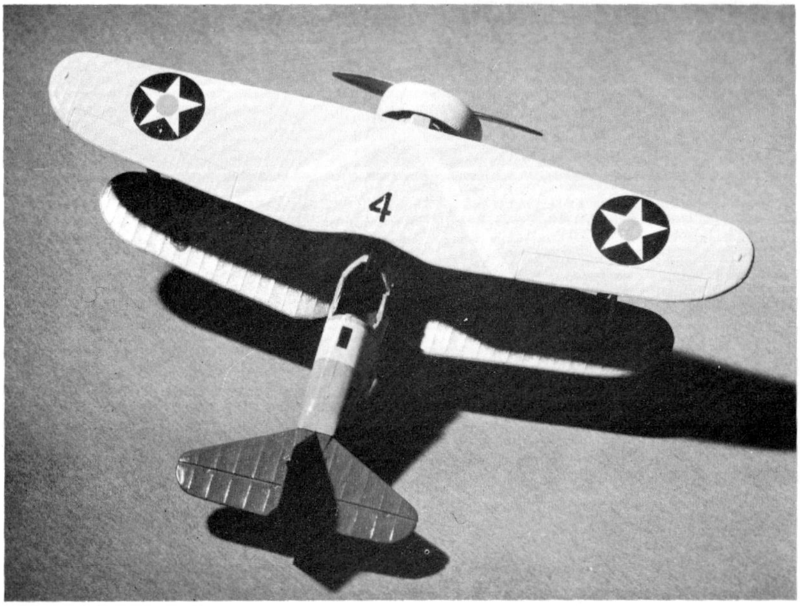

46

An orange-red filter was used here to suppress the yellow of the upper wing.

reason, we want to make the white band on the top wing in fig. **46** stand out less than it does, we select a filter that will lighten the orange-yellow. In this case an orange filter gave the best results.

Artificial light by itself, by virtue of its 'redness', does not give a very good rendering of this yellow in any case, and if we really want to improve matters, we must bring back some of the blue. The light blue conversion filter darkened the yellow sufficiently. Please take note that, if we filter too strongly, the results are likely to be unrealistic. If we use a dark blue filter in the case of fig. **47**, we may end up with a very dark grey top wing, while the tail, which was red in the model, will turn a solid black.

Another type of filter we often have to use is the polarisation filter. In marked contrast with colour correction filters, we cannot afford to

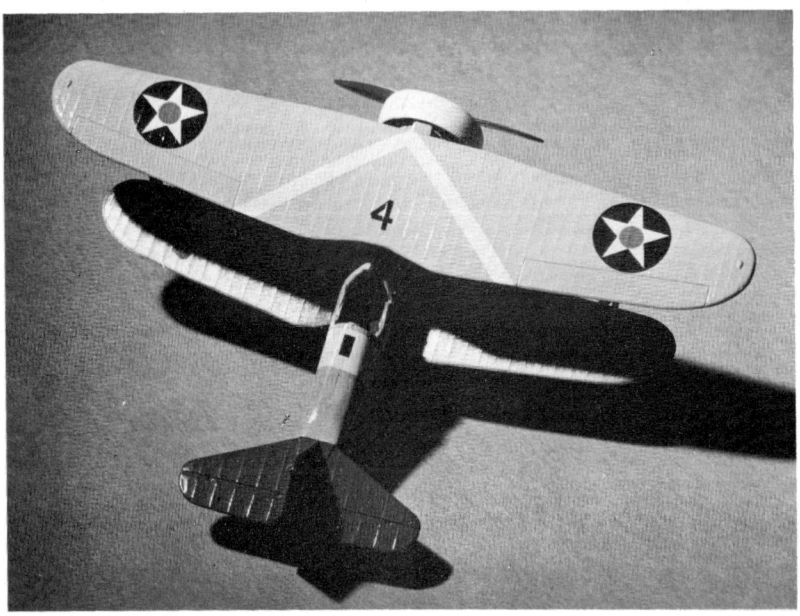

47

A light blue filter, converting tungsten light to daylight, darkens the yellow sufficiently to make the white band stand out.

B

AB=unpolarized light; BC=reflected and polarized light; P=polarizing filter, which can be turned in a plane perpendicular to BC and which can regulate the intensity of CE. At the angle of 57° shown here we can eliminate CE completely, in other words, 'cut out' a reflection. KS=a reflecting surface. This can be anything but a metal.

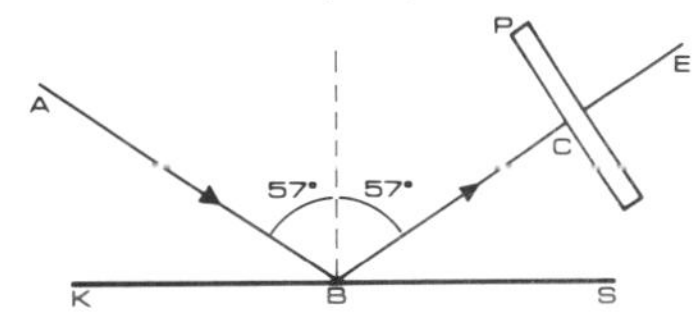

look upon these as a mere luxury. We will soon find that we have to use them practically all the time, certainly from the moment we start using plate glass in our settings. Luckily only one of these filters is all we need: most camera manufacturers have had the good sense to design most of their lenses to accept the same size filter. This certainly applies to the range of lenses we are using, say 28mm-50mm; longer tele-photo lenses are probably larger in diameter. Polarisation filters are quite expensive, but they will soon prove their worth.

To illustrate this, we took a series of photographs, both with and without pola filter, as shown in figs. **48-50**. The improvements will be fairly obvious, and these are exactly the little things we run into every time we photograph a model.

Polarisation filters eliminate reflections for the full 100% only at the angle of 57°, as shown in diagram **B**, and then only on surfaces such as glass, varnish, glossy paint, etc. No such luck with metals. They are usually supplied in a double rotating ring, which enables us to turn the filter round whilst screwed on the lens, and select the position in which reflections are completely suppressed. The fact that these filters are fully effective only at that particular angle, limits to a certain extent the ways in which we can take our pictures. If, when looking into the viewfinder, we find that the offenders are still there, even though much reduced in intensity, a slight adjustment of the camera angle will often have the desired effect.

The finish on many scale models is more glossy than it was on the original and pola filters can be used very effectively to cut distracting highlights. Semi-matt and even matt surfaces can pick up a surprising amount of shine, depending on how we have arranged our lights. Often on a fuselage side, which is otherwise correctly illuminated, the decals spoil everything with ghastly reflections.

We mentioned plate glass — fig. **51** is an ex-

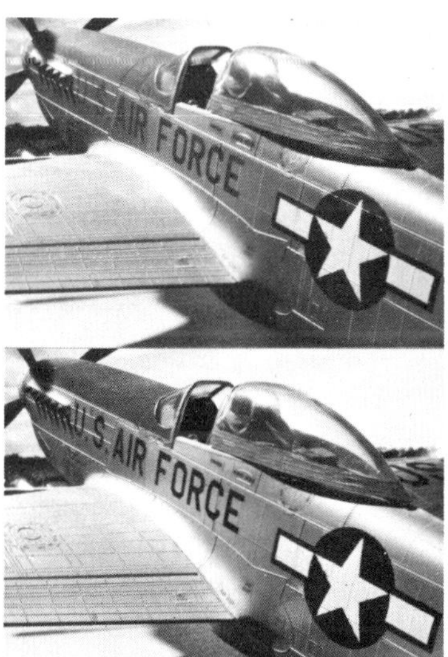

48

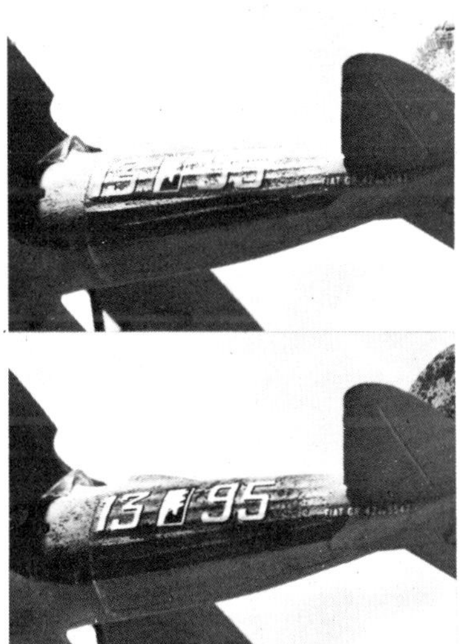

49

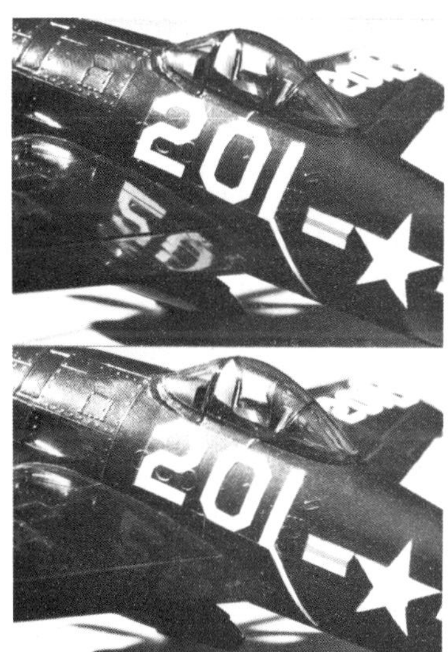

50

ample of thıs treatment. The model is placed on a sheet of glass, preferably plate glass, 6mm thick, which in turn is supported a short distance above whatever background we choose. The success of this method, of which we will give more details later, depends entirely on our ability to eliminate any reflections, of which there will be plenty, especially if the background we use is dark in colour, as in fig. **51**. Armed with our polarisation filters, properly adjusted, we have the aircraft as we intended it, floating in the air (fig. **52**). The slightest trace of reflections in a picture as this fill give our game away.

A dark reflection, however, will not show up against a lighter background. This can be noted even in fig. **51**, where virtually no reflections are visible against the white markings on the ground. This is a very welcome discovery, as it gives us another means of controlling unwanted reflections. By manipulating the brightness of the entire background in a setting where this is possible, we can eliminate most reflections; at least we will have rendered them invisible. This course of action is not always possible; if the background is meant to be darker, as it was in figs. **51** and **52**, we obviously can not lighten it to any great extent. Sky backgrounds, on the other hand, are always lighter than our objects,

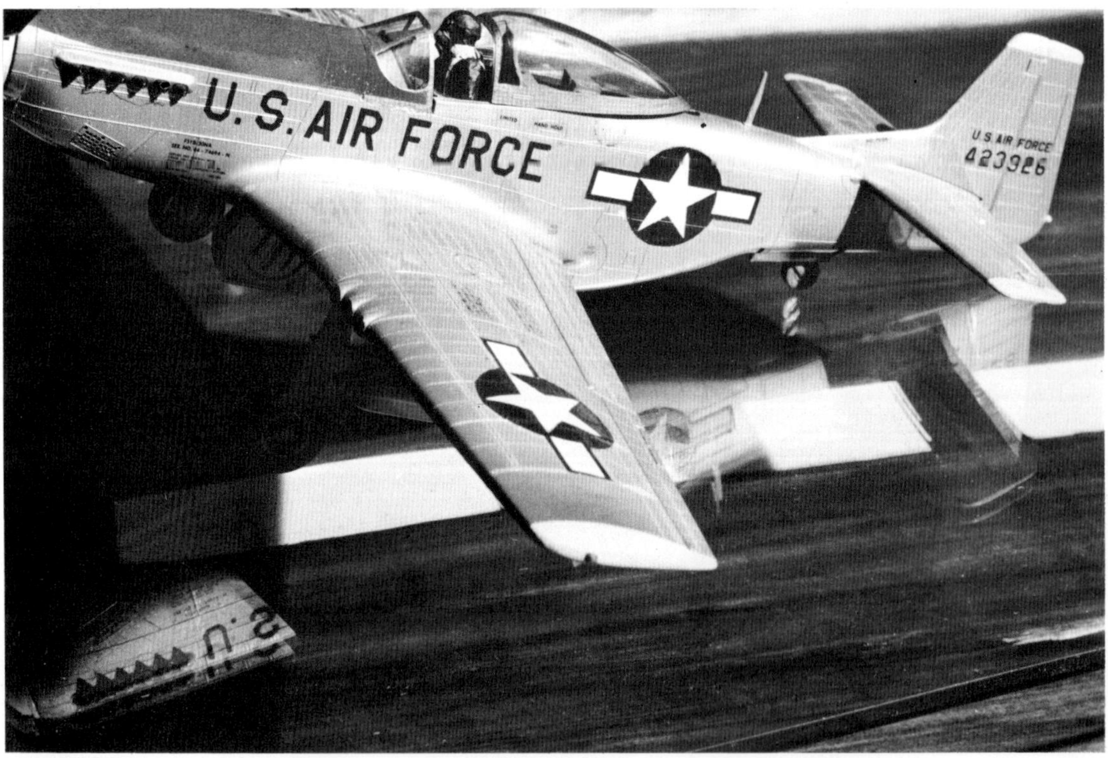

51

and we can apply this technique to our hearts' content.

We may encounter problems that can not be solved by this method, however, if we illuminate our model from behind. This results in the brightest parts of it facing the glass, and so our reflections will be bright. To overcome this, we can increase the amount of light on the background to a point where it overpowers the reflection, if this is feasible; should this fail, we have no option but to revert to the old brush-and-matt-black-paint trick, in other words, we will paint everything that could possibly cause a bright reflection, matt black, provided always that these parts are on the other side of our model and therefore invisible to the camera. We can use a black poster colour for this purpose and wash everything clean after completion of our mission.

This procedure is practicable only where we have our model between camera and glass plate; if we work from underneath the glass, looking through it, there will be no reflections, at least not of any part of the model. We may be surprised to find any part of the background reflected in the underside of the glass, which of course causes more problems, and more serious ones at that. The remedy in this case is usually found in the use of large sheets of black paper, stuck over

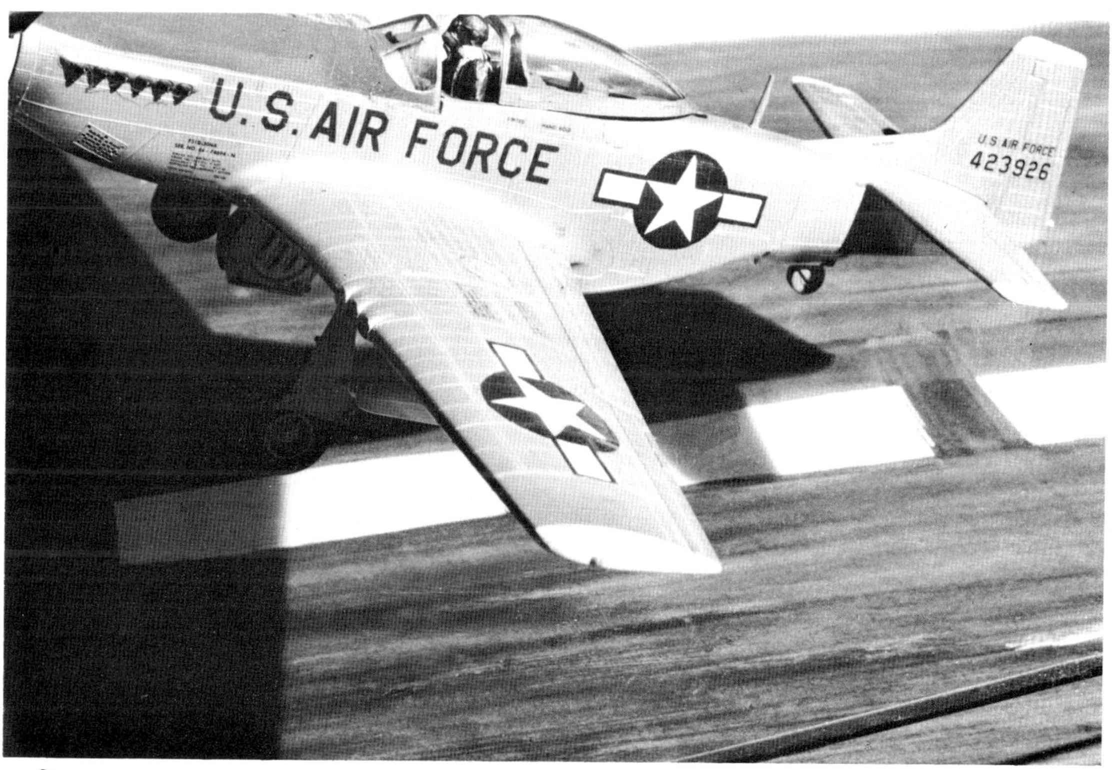

52

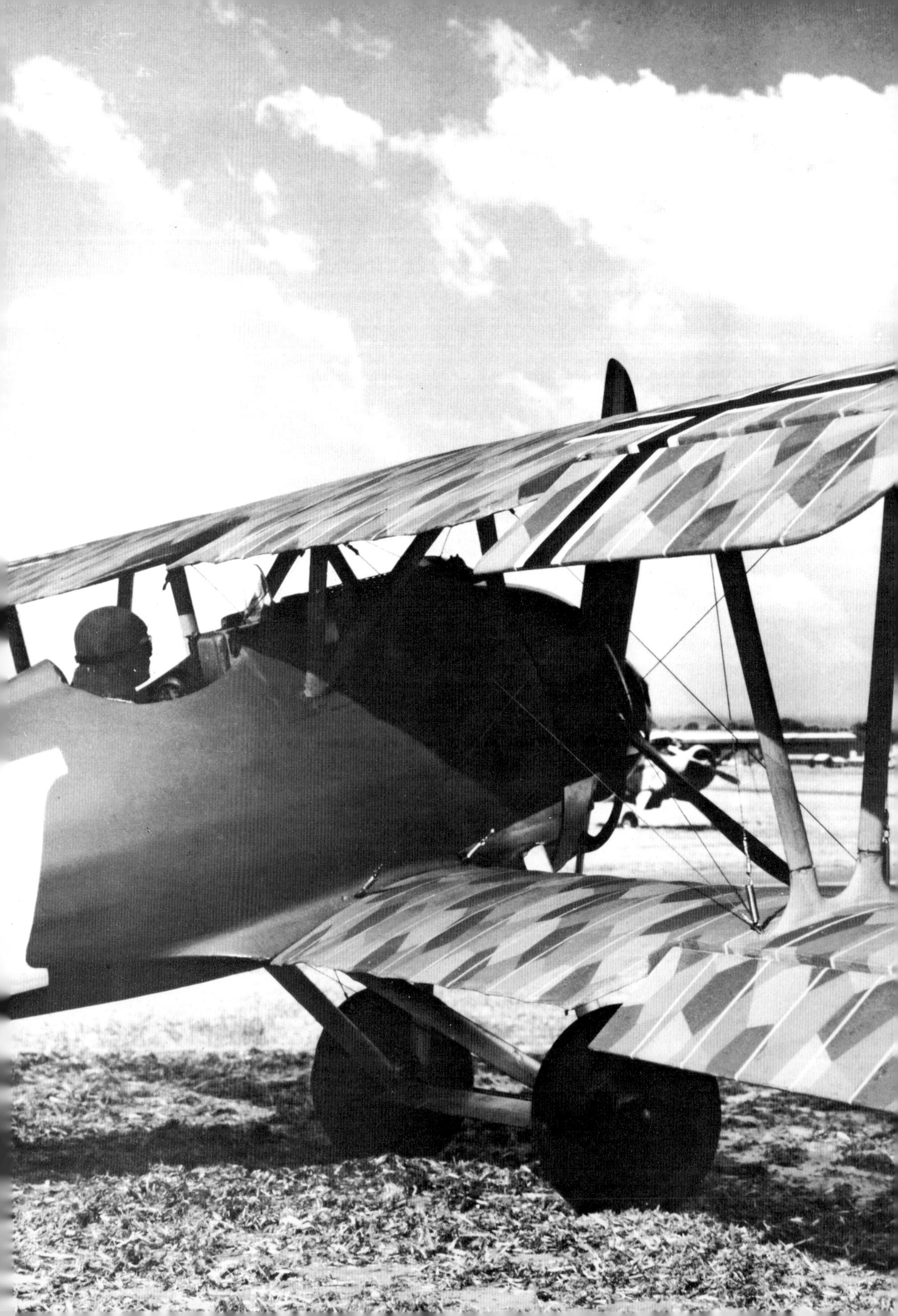

54 On modern panchromatic film all the subtle nuances of the Lozenge-pattern are lost; compare this with results we got on (old-fashioned) orthochromatic film, fig. 53. Notice also how the tones of fuselage, cowling and wheel covers are reversed.

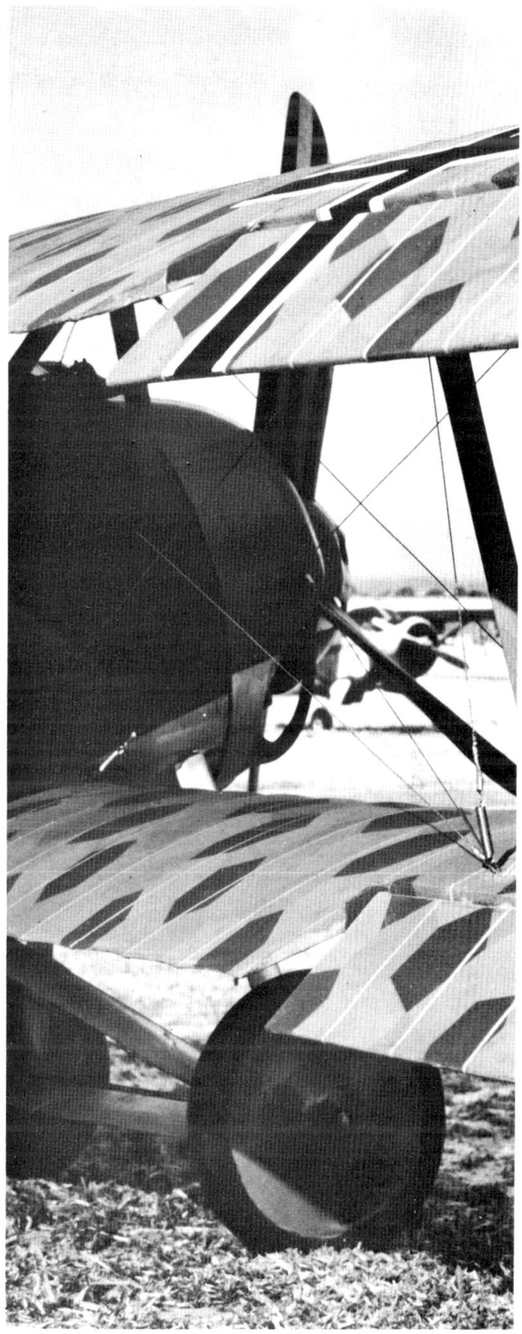

those parts of the background not actually forming part of the scene to be photographed.

In all these cases, as well as in many others, properly managed lighting, together with a carefully used pola filter, will spell the difference between failure and success.

Our last exercise is only vaguely related to the experiments with filters. In fig. **53** we have a veteran of WWI, the SSW-DIII, built as a flying model to 1/9 scale (free flight) and painted in the authentic colours. Of these aircraft not many photographs were taken and certainly very few have survived to see this day. The vast majority are of a rather poor quality; photography itself was only in its infancy and moreover there was a war on. The point is, however, that whatever pictures were taken in those days, they were taken on ortho-chromatic film, which was the only film available then. This film, as the name implies, was sensitive only to blue, green and yellow and quite insensitive to red. The resulting photographs showed the by now famous lozenge-pattern of these German fighters in anything but its true grey-value.

We can do the same thing today, because ortho-chromatic film is still being made, albeit for the professional photographer, who uses it for reproductions of black and white continuous-tone originals. The result is a very pleasing description of the pattern; every individual shape is clearly visible. In terms of correct tone-rendering they are all wrong of course, but the effect is quite attractive nevertheless.

The same shot on modern pan-chromatic film strikes us as an anti-climax. Of the four colours used in this lozenge-pattern, three have exactly the same grey-value, while one is a fraction darker. The three merge into one grey mass (fig. **54**), leaving the darker one standing out. Note also the difference in tone-rendering of the cowling and wheel discs (bright red) and the fuselage (blue). We used a 4" x 5" technical camera for this shot; see also diagram **C**, page 41, for more technical information.

CHAPTER

6 AIRBORNE!

Until now we have occupied ourselves mainly with clearing the ground in preparation for bigger things to come. We did get a few glimpses of these here and there, without going into any great detail. We will now grasp the nettle firmly, however, and put our knowledge of the basic principles to the test. The first few examples are still fairly simple, but as we go further, these will become more and more complicated.

In fig. **55** we have an aircraft parked on an airfield; this particular one, the SSW-DIII, we have already met a short while ago, and the setting itself is also familiar. Diagram **C** shows the principle of the set-up in more detail. Throughout the remainder of this book, we will use the same symbols to indicate flood- and spotlights, as well as the relevant positions of the camera, together with the appropriate angles of field. We have taken the liberty to assume that all cameras are always firmly mounted on a sturdy tripod and we have therefore deleted the latter from the diagrams.

About the only difficulty in a set-up as shown in fig. **55**, is finding the correct position of the horizon. Since all the panels on which we have mounted our backgrounds and surfaces are of necessity mobile, we have to be very careful when preparing the set for a new model. In real life the position of the horizon in our photographs depends solely on the direction in which we point our camera: drop it to just above ground level and the horizon drops with it; raise it to say, 200ft and the horizon may not even be in the picture, depending on how far downwards we point the camera. The horizon should never be confused with the skyline: in a valley, with mountains all around, the skyline will be way above us, while the horizon, although not visible, is low down. If we hoist ourselves to the top of the nearest mountain, we will witness how skyline and horizon are now virtually coinciding. Pilots make good use of this knowledge: if they spot another aircraft, its position in relation to the horizon tells them whether it is flying above or below their own aircraft, no matter at what altitude they are themselves.

Based on the very same principle is the following extremely useful rule, which works as follows: we are looking at our (real) aircraft; our eyes are at a certain distance from the ground we are standing on, say 2M, to keep things nice and easy, albeit a bit tall perhaps; we can also see the horizon, although we may have to estimate its exact position.

We notice that our aircraft and the horizon intersect at a certain spot: this spot now is also 2m. above the ground. The explanation is that a line from our eye to the horizon is a horizontal line, and all points on a horizontal line are at the same distance from the ground, assuming of course, that the ground is horizontal. This provides us with an eminently practical means of finding the correct position of the horizon when we are taking a picture of our model. If we know for instance, that the top of the fin stands 1.95m above ground, then all we have to do is make sure that this top sits a little bit below the horizon, that is, below our viewing height. We calculate a normal viewing height at the scale of our model, e.g. at 1/72 scale we will have to find a way to position the camera at some 25mm from the table top. This distance is always measured from the optical axis of the lens, which no doubt presents a new problem: the average size of today's 35mm camera is such, that the distance from the bottom of the camera to the centre line through the lens is about 35-40mm, making it difficult to lower the camera to 25mm. The solution is to cut the ground just in front of the camera, or, alternatively, to put the camera very close to the edge of the board, in such a way that the distance between it and the centre of the lens is the desired 25mm.

A small object can be made to look enormous by moving very close to it and staying very close to the ground. Such a shot would be somewhat unrealistic, apart from being extremely difficult. Equally wrong is it, to photograph a

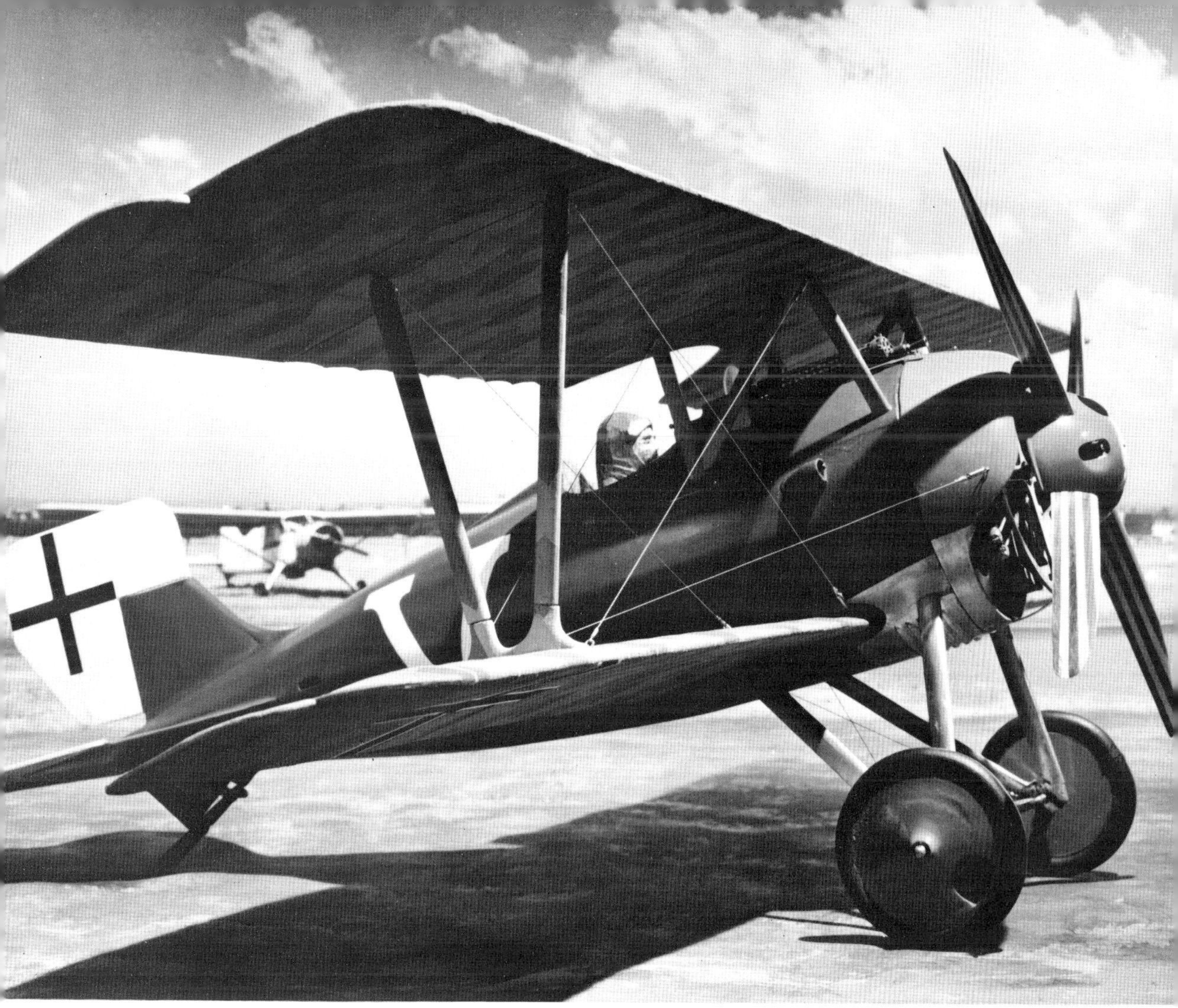

large aircraft as if it were a tiny one, and this is a mistake which is easily and very often made. To go to the first extreme, one would have to be in the possession of an extreme wide-angle lens, able to focus at close range. Most people seem to have a tendency to stay as far away from what they are photographing as they possibly can. The best results, however, are obtained if we photograph scale models from 'scale viewpoints', which means that we do have to move in pretty close in most cases.

Another aid in finding the horizon, especially when working with biplanes, is to extend the lines of the top and bottom wing. These will of necessity have to meet at a vanishing point on the horizon, because such are the laws of nature. Be careful with that particular model you are taking pictures of: if no dihedral is present in either wing, things are quite simple. Just view at the leading edge of a wing across any straight-edge of sufficient length, and memorize the spot

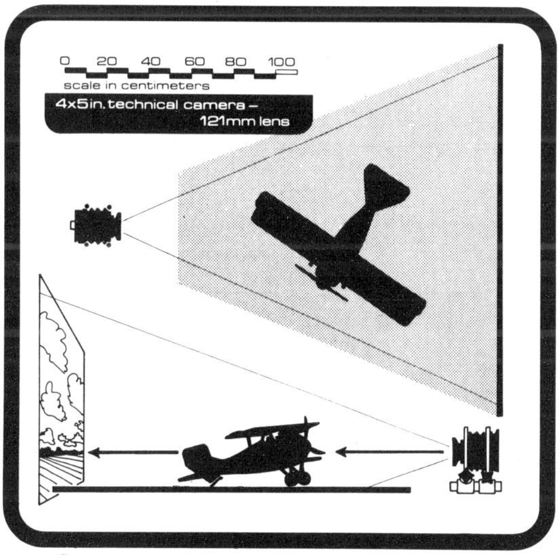

C

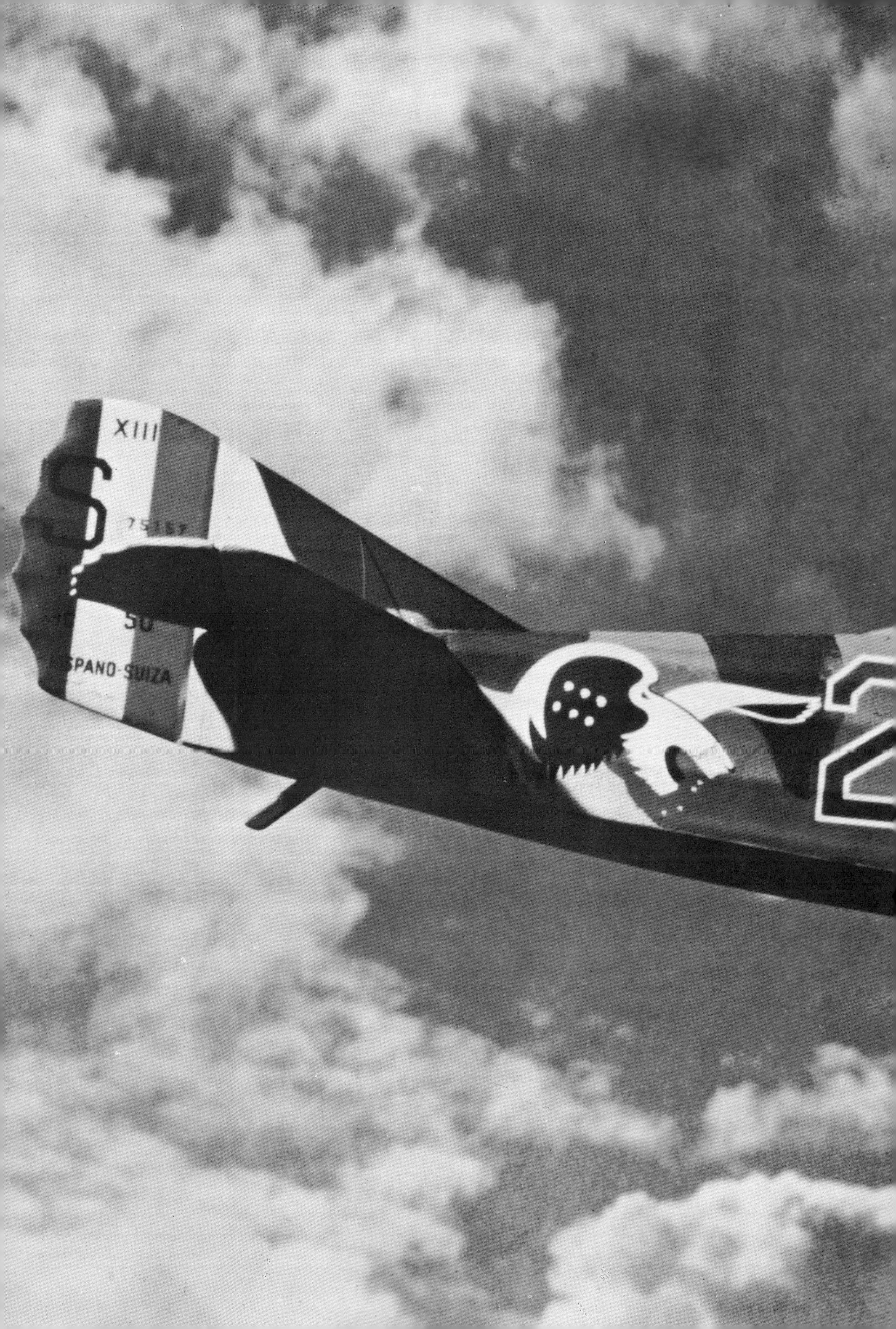
XIII
S
75157
50
SPANO-SUIZA

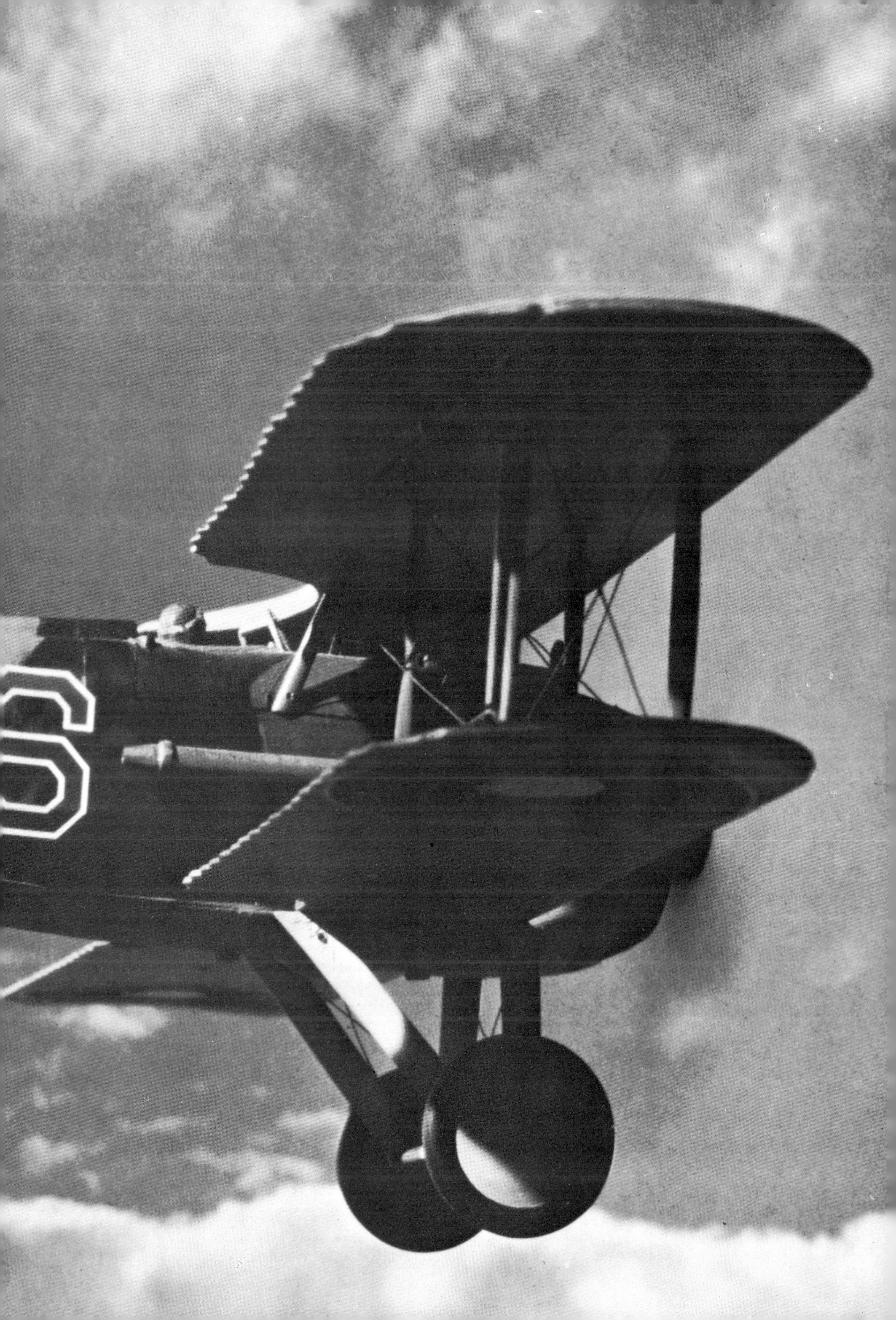

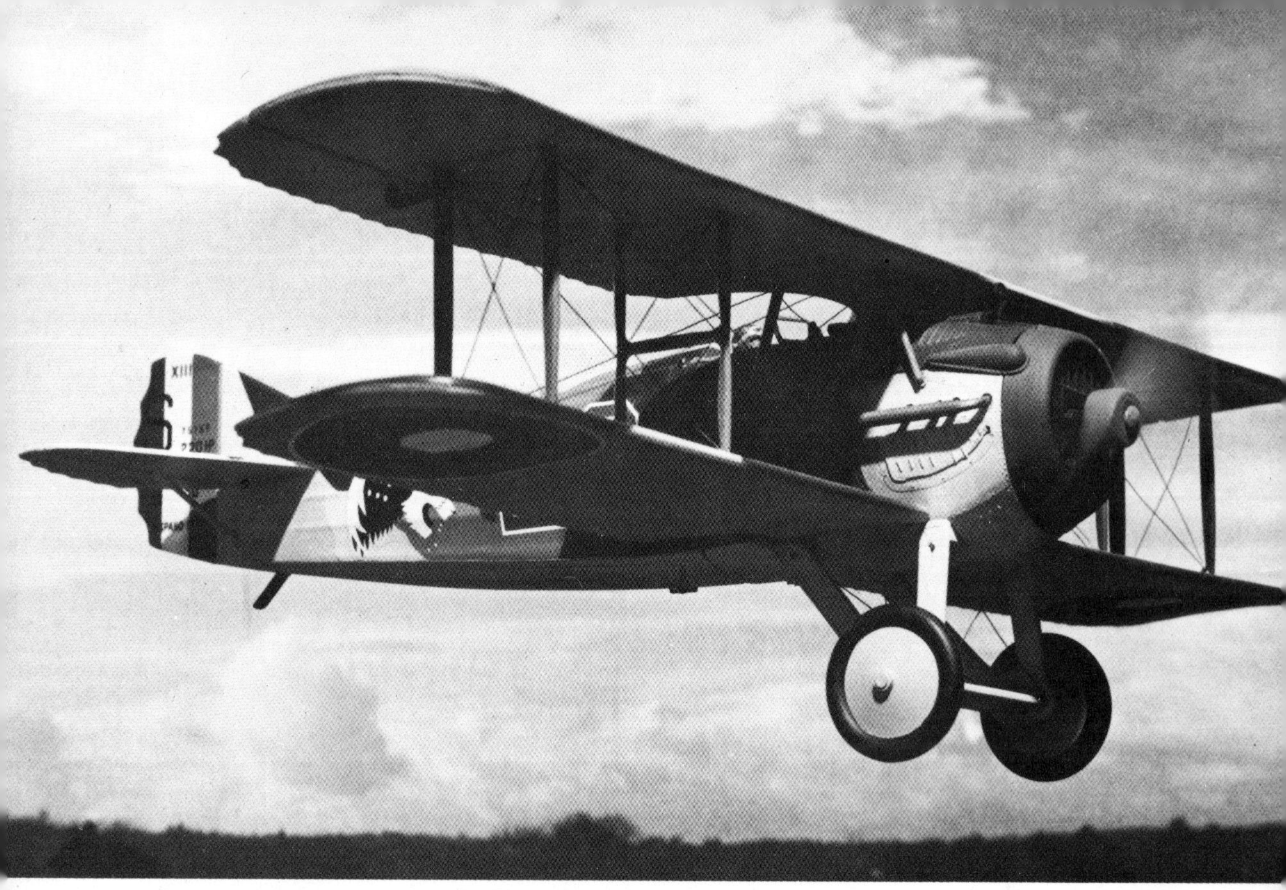

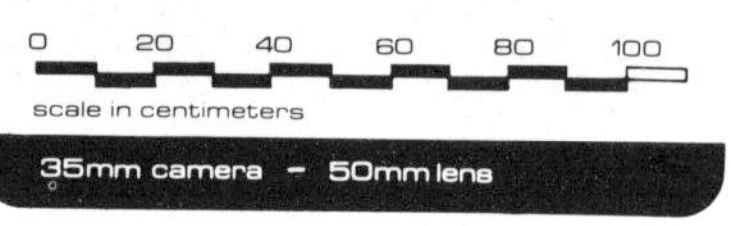

It is sometimes possible to illuminate both model and background with just one spotlight, as illustrated here. It is, however, advisable to place this single light as far away as possible in order to minimise uneven lighting of the background. Be also on your guard for the shadow of the model itself, which may on no account fall onto the background.

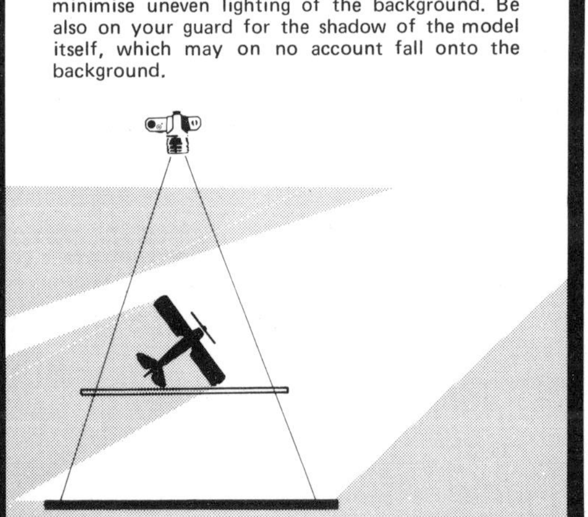

D

where it seems to meet the horizon. Repeat this procedure with the other wing: if this line meets the horizon at the same spot, your horizon is in the right position; if it does not, you will have to adjust it in such a way, that this vanishing point falls on it. On no account can a vanishing point be located above the skyline, while the aircraft is standing on a horizontal surface. Be very particular, when carrying out all this viewing, to be in exactly the same spot as where the camera will be. Better still is to view through the camera, although this presents other problems, because then our straight-line will be partly in-, and partly out of focus.

If your plane has wings with dihedral, which will be the case with most post-WWI aircraft, extend the lines across the tips of the wings.

As we mentioned earlier, finding the correct position of the horizon in relation to our model is very important. A study of photographs of similar aircraft in real life will give you a good idea of this.

Once the model is placed on a surface, care must be taken to blend the tone of this surface (hereafter to be referred to as the ground) into the tone of the bottom part of the background where it meets the ground. Where this turns out to be difficult, we can use our lights to make them appear in the same tone. If we arrange our floodlights to illuminate the vertical background, then some light will spill over on the ground; the vertical part receives much more light than the horizontal ground. If we start with both of these having the same tone, then under these lighting conditions the vertical part will appear much lighter than the ground. Consequently, if we have a ground which is lighter in tone than the vertical background, we can correct this situation with our lights alone. We may need additional spotlights to make the ground appear

E

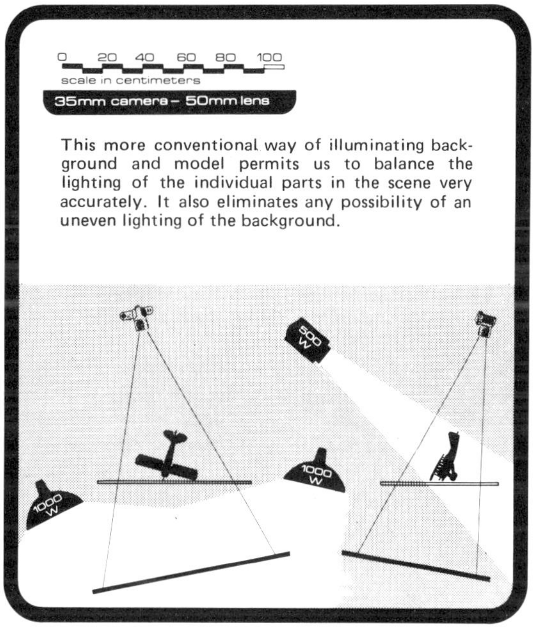

This more conventional way of illuminating background and model permits us to balance the lighting of the individual parts in the scene very accurately. It also eliminates any possibility of an uneven lighting of the background.

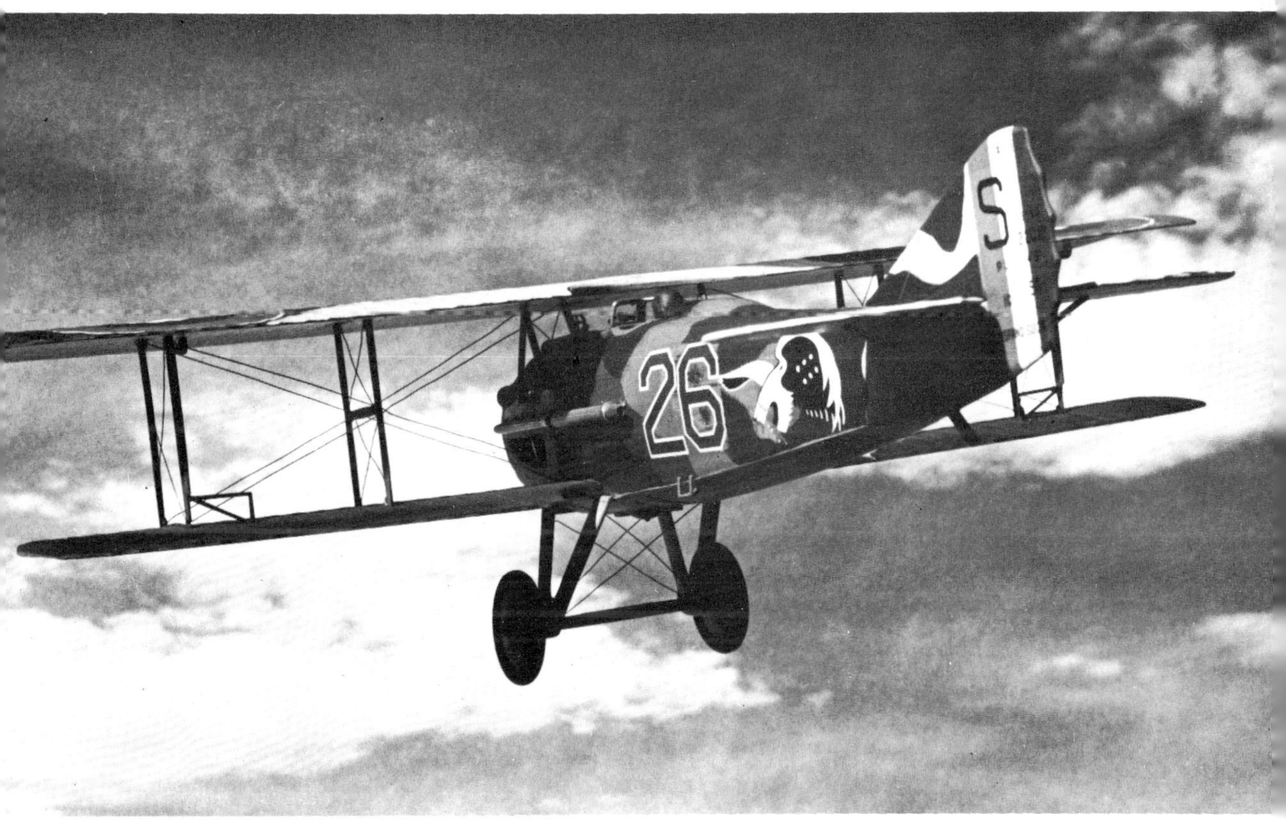

57

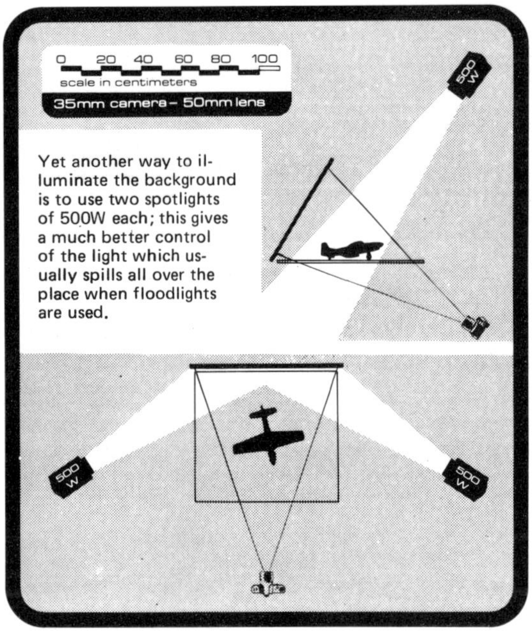

F

the right tone if the latter happens to be darker than the vertical background.

For a background with clouds to be really effective, it must be lit in such a way, that any object with a surface tone other than very light, stands out against it darker than the sky itself. The lightest part of the sky is always the area near the horizon; the presence of haze reduces the intensity of the deep blue of the overhead (cloudless) sky and even an overcast sky is usually lighter in this region. Towards the top we can let it go as dark as we like; this actually gives a strong feeling of distance.

Many photographs of models are taken with the model placed on a suitable surface outside; this has to have a structure sufficiently fine to be in harmony with the model. Whilst all our lighting problems would be instantly solved this way, the problem of scale remains, particularly where it concerns the background and other objects we cannot avoid. Invariably objects close by appear much too large and there is no remedy for this. A horizon in the far distance will more than likely match the model in scale, but our depth of field will have to extend from a point some distance in front of our model, to all the way back in infinity. This is too much to ask of many lenses; in a studio setting we have to bridge a gap of only 1-1.50m.

Having dealt with stationary aircraft, we will now proceed to the moving, or flying ones. These are easier in so far that no ground is involved; we have only one surface to illuminate. The large blown-up photographs of clouds present a problem for the average amateur photographer. Finding a suitable sky and getting that on negative is generally not too hard, but blowing that negative up to say, a 2m wide print, is a different story. In most cases one would have to resort to one of the many professional people to get this done. Photographic prints will have to be mounted flat to avoid unsightly wrinkles. Even the surface known as semi-matt reflects a fair amount of light; the more matt the prints are, the less trouble we will encounter. An alternative method is shown in diagram **F**, page 46, where two spotlights were used to light the background. These can be kept at a greater distance from the set, their light is more intense, they do not spill so much light and are generally easier to handle. They are also a lot more expensive.

If a light is allowed to reflect directly off the paper, we will get a practically unprintable negative, or, even worse, a pure white area in our transparency, due to gross over-exposure of the reflecting part. Fortunately we can see exactly what we are doing in our SLR cameras, and we will soon discover that we are spending more time trouble-shooting than we do taking the actual picture. It may take the best part of an hour to set up something that looks promising; after all that hard work, it would be utterly foolish to take only one or two negatives, particularly when working with black and white film. Try out different exposures: it will require some practising under actual working conditions to get everything timed properly, especially if our propeller is not of the cooperative kind.

Figs. **56**, **57** and **58** show the tricks we can play with the old biplane. The fact that upper and lower wing are practically the same length on the SPAD allowed us to put the model on its side; this unfortunately is something we can do with very few other aircraft.

We almost forgot to mention that in the

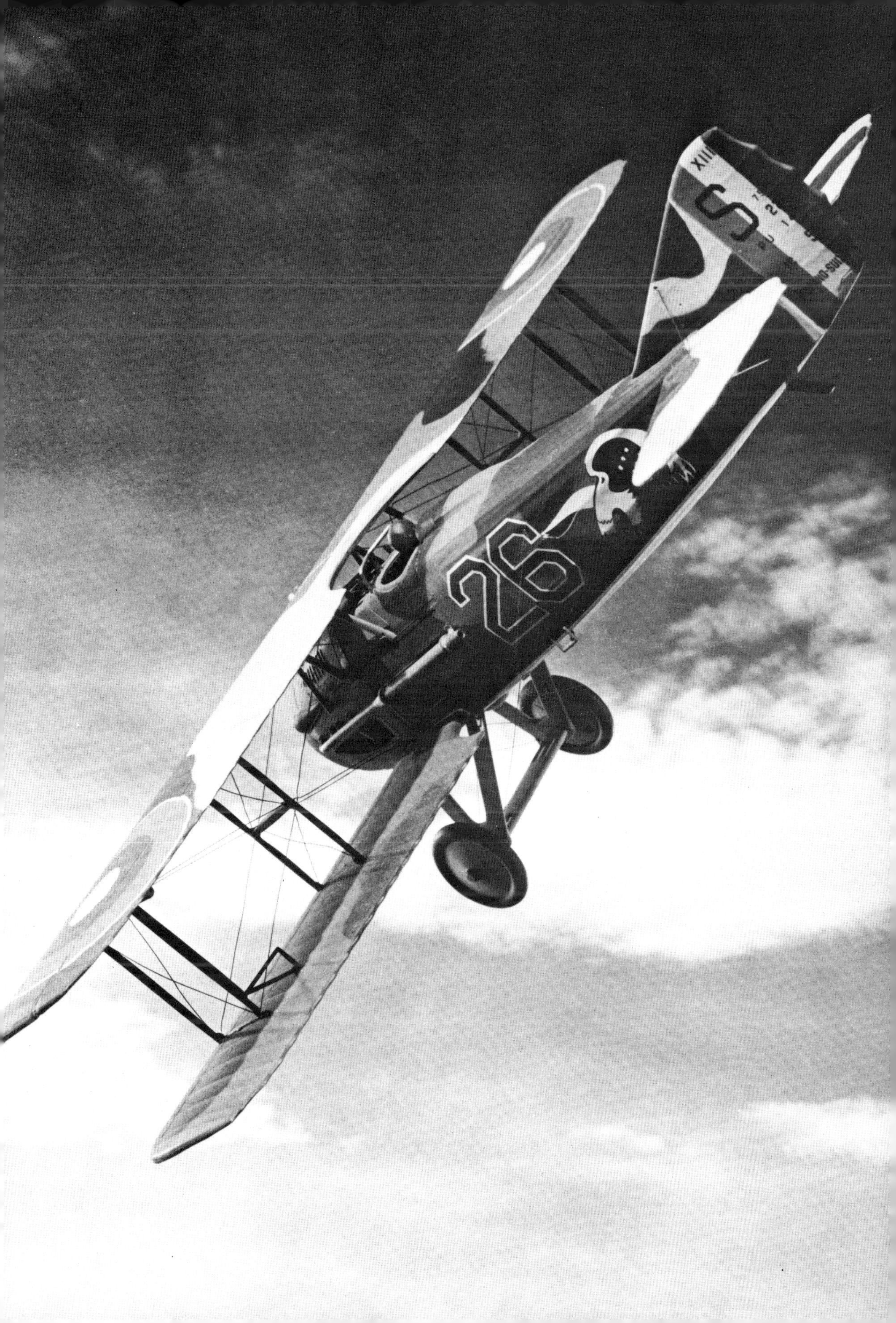
XIII
26

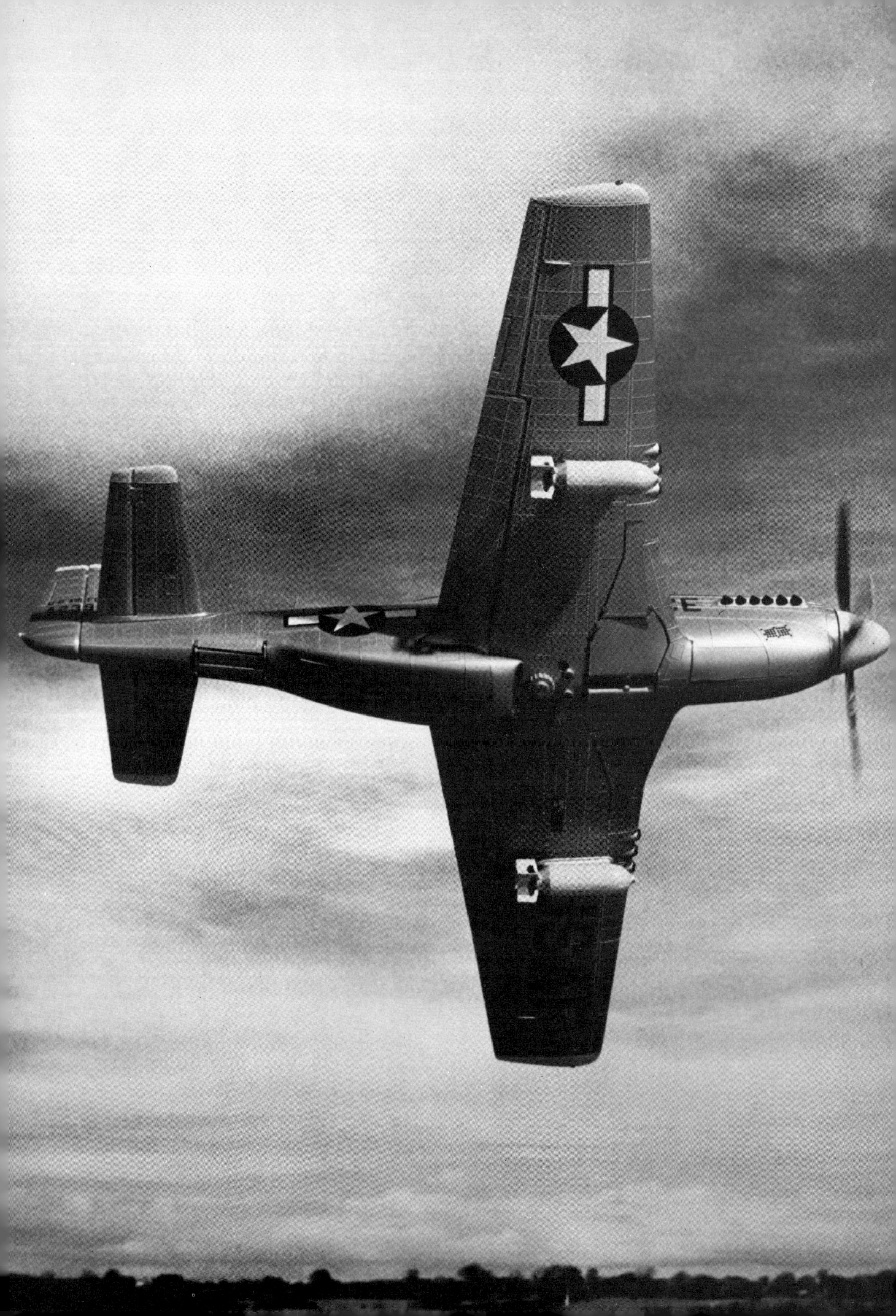

G

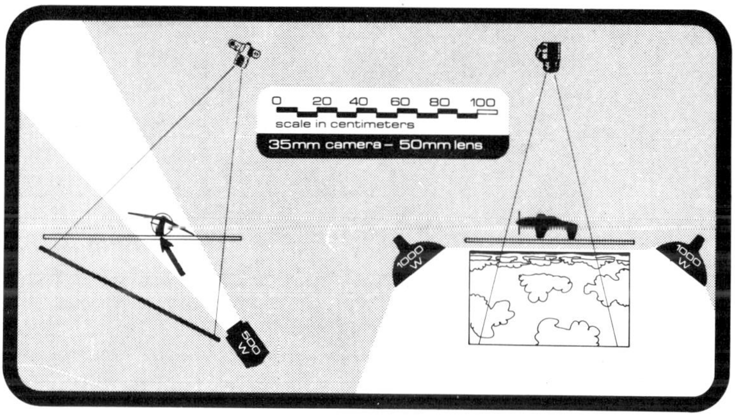

In this setting everything is turned upside down to allow the propeller to turn - model is propped up from below (see arrow) for this reason.

meantime we have progressed to using the glass-plate; this priceless piece of equipment makes possible many a picture we would only be dreaming about otherwise. In fig. **56** (diagram **D**) the model was resting on its wingtips and tailplane; in fig. **57** (diagram **E**) it was tipped on its nose and a wingtip: the propeller was omitted since it could not possibly turn around and the hub was invisible anyway. A moving propeller, seen from directly in front or from behind, is virtually impossible to see.

In fig. **58** the model rests on its nose, as in fig. **57**; note how with exactly the same means, the picture has much more impact, simply by selecting a different viewpoint and and generally turning the complete set around a bit. Before you realize it, you will be at the end of your 36 exposures!

In the diagrams we have indicated the wattage of each light. 1000W floodlights, complete with stands, would require a fairly large capital outlay. A 500W spotlight, however, which is by no means a large one, will cost you even more. Our photographs can be taken with a good deal less

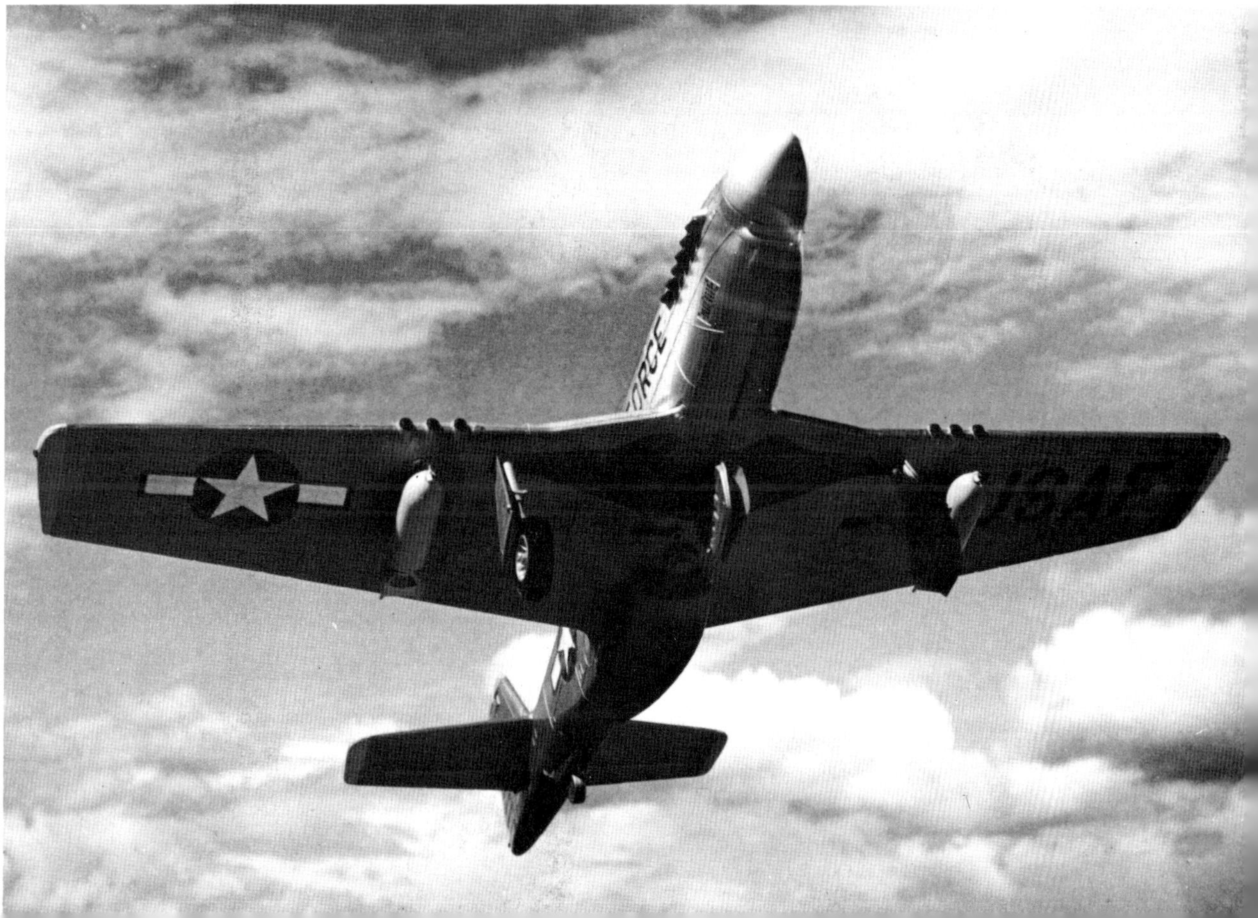

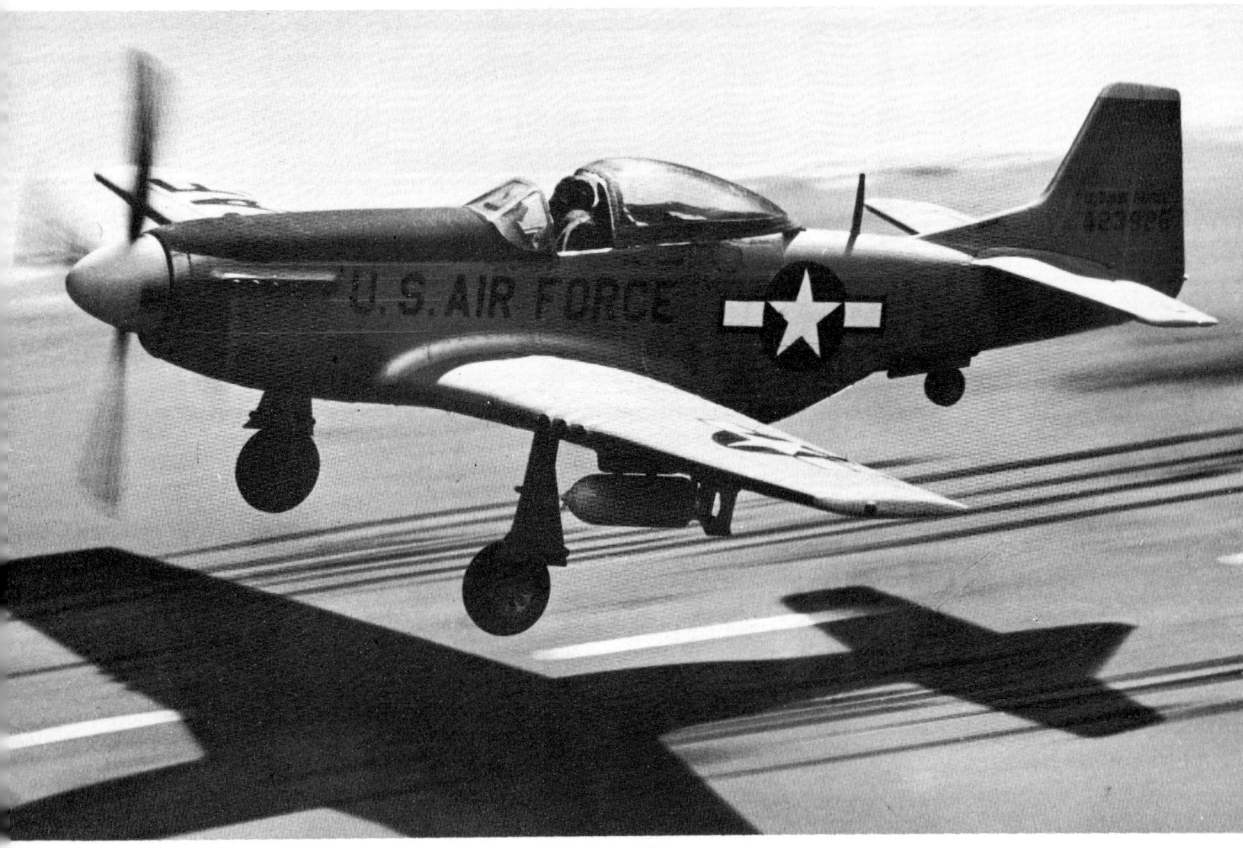

In plan A the large arrow indicates the camera direction; the bold dotted line shows the trapezoidal area which appears ultimately as a horizontal rectangle in our picture. This explains why we have to include so much ground *behind* our model to fill the entire frame. The small arrows show the amount of movement during the exposure necessary to render the ground 'blurred'. Section B shows how the glass plate was raised at the back to obtain the required position.

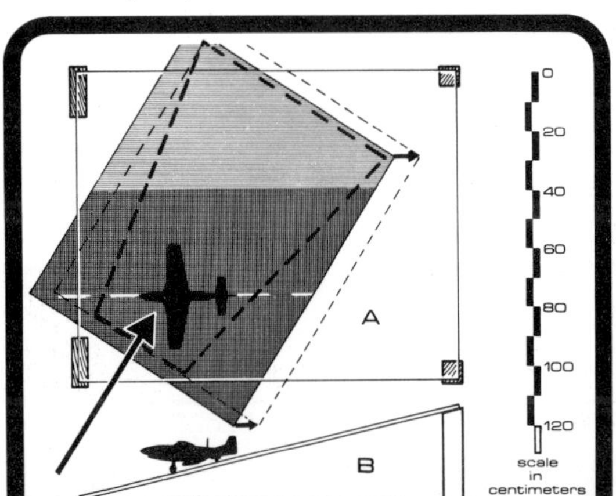

H

light; we can for instance divide the wattage of each light by 2 (or 4), which gives us 500W for the floodlights and 250W for the spotlight (or 250W and 125W respectively).

The problem is not so much the total amount of light we can throw on a set, although this does determine the exposure time; it is more a question of how to distribute it properly. By varying the distance between lights and objects we can control the illumination to a very fine degree; it is roughly speaking inversely proportional to the distance (double the distance, half the light) for large light sources such as floodlights and inversely proportional to the square of the distance for small ones such as spotlights (double the distance, one-quarter the light).

Fig. **59** presented us with a totally new problem: the model, put down on its underbelly, turned out to be so low, that it was impossible to turn the propeller. We turned the entire set upside-down, including the sky, and propped the model up from underneath to clear the propeller;

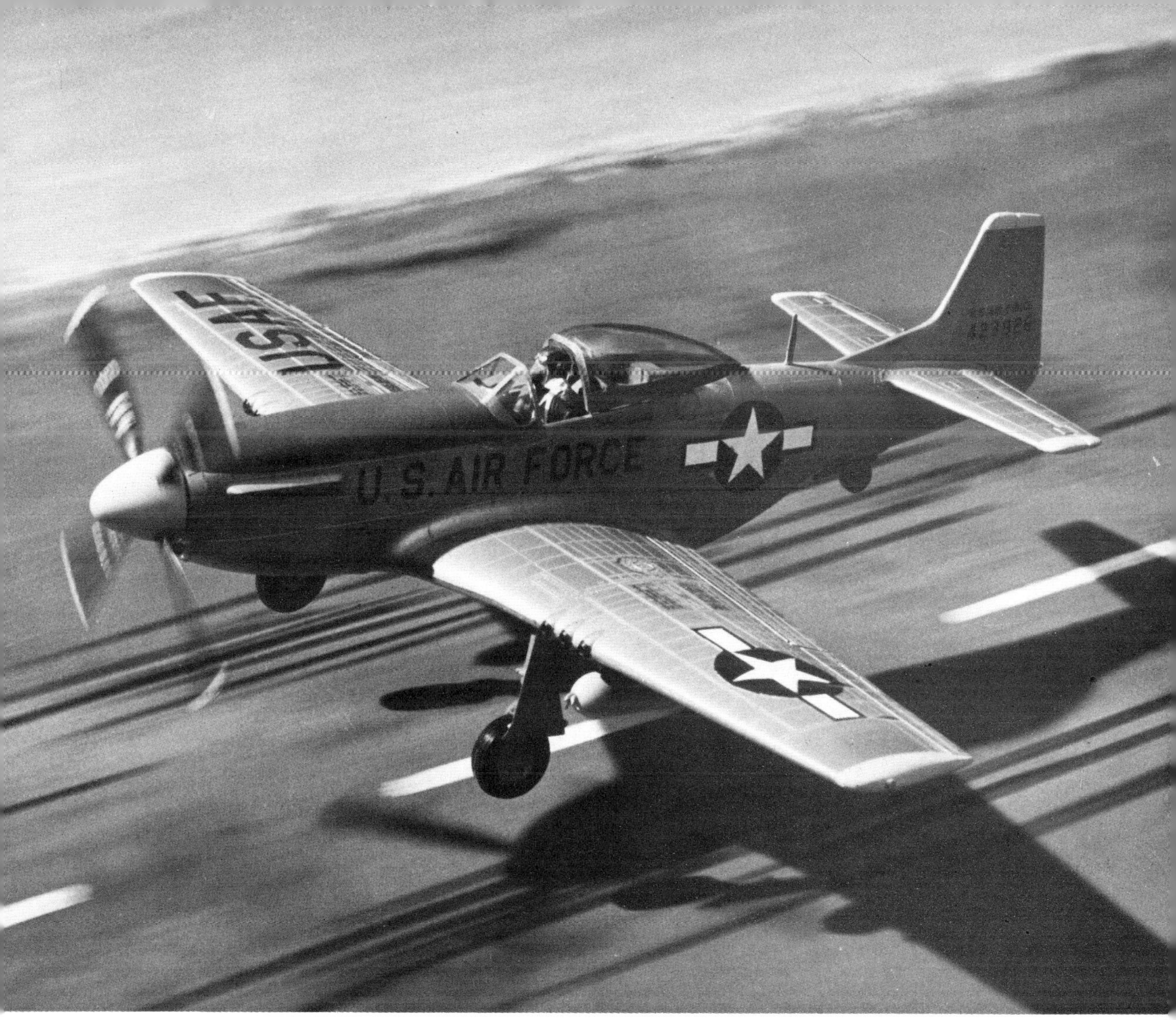
USAF
U.S. AIR FORCE

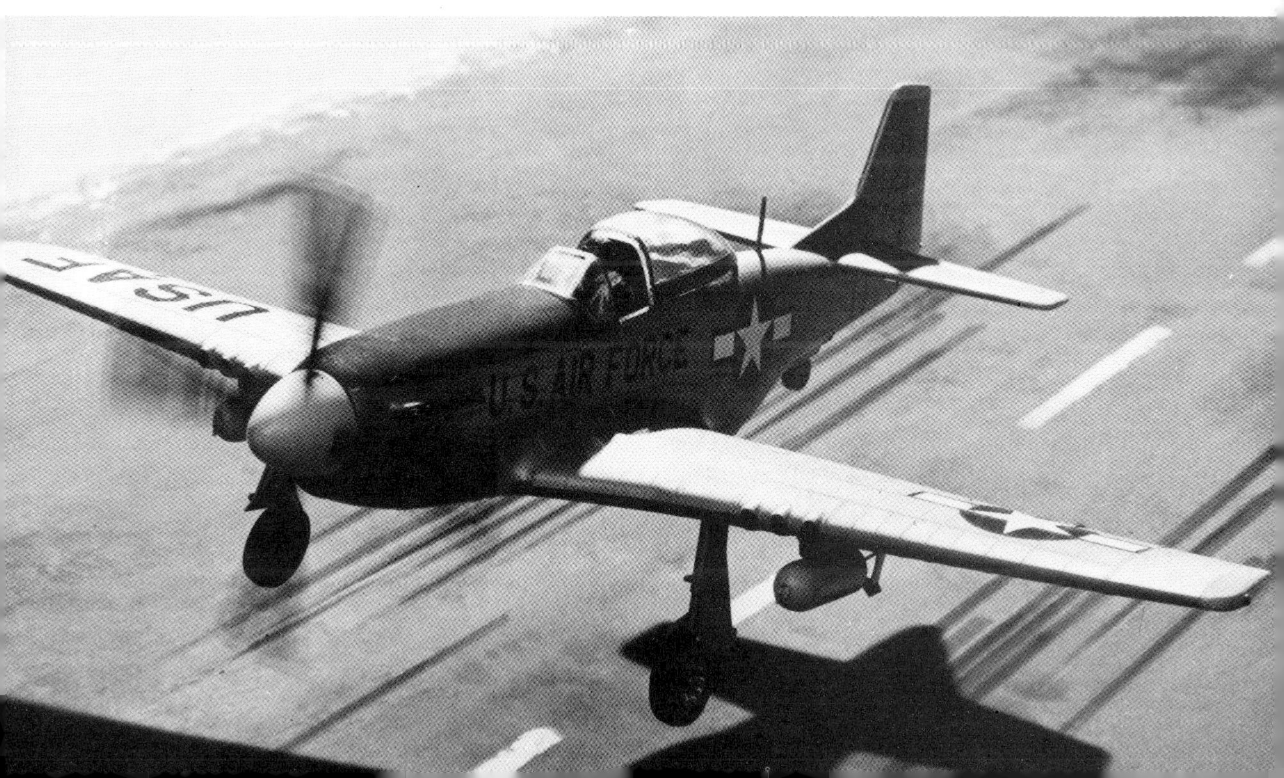
USAF
U.S. AIR FORCE

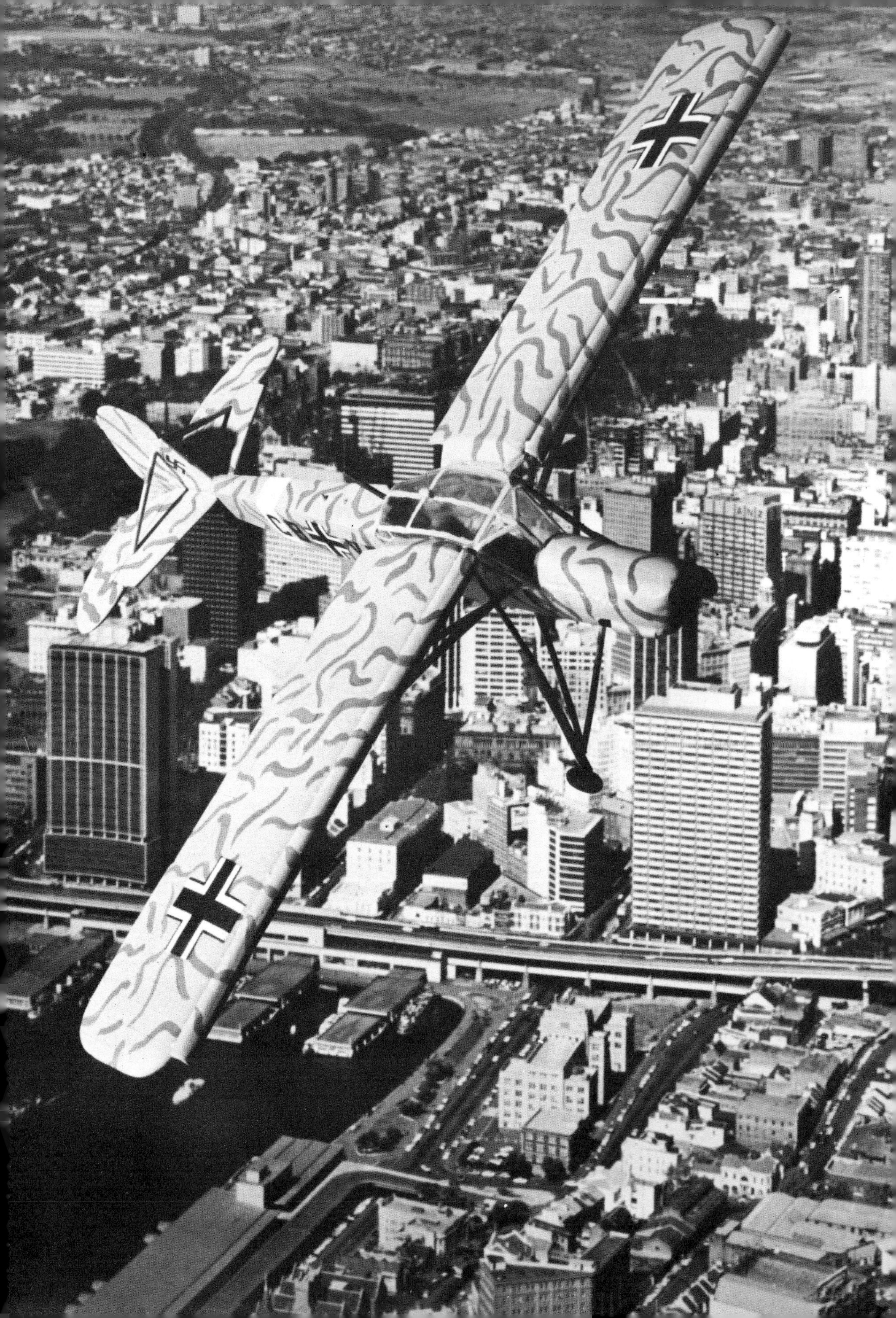

the appropriate position of the spotlight is explained in diagram **G**.

Fig. **60** is taken from below the glass plate, the model standing on its undercarriage as it should. The two inner wheel doors, which were flapping wildly as we blew on the prop, have been taped together with a minute piece of transparent tape. A distinctly irritating feature of this kind of set-up is the reflection of the main light in the glass: this light itself does not become visible, but we will find the underside of the model illuminated in a most unpleasant manner. Diagram

I

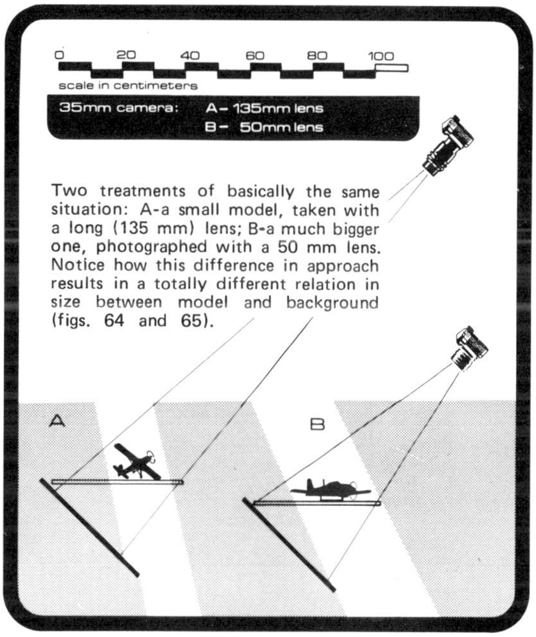

Two treatments of basically the same situation: A-a small model, taken with a long (135 mm) lens; B-a much bigger one, photographed with a 50 mm lens. Notice how this difference in approach results in a totally different relation in size between model and background (figs. 64 and 65).

65

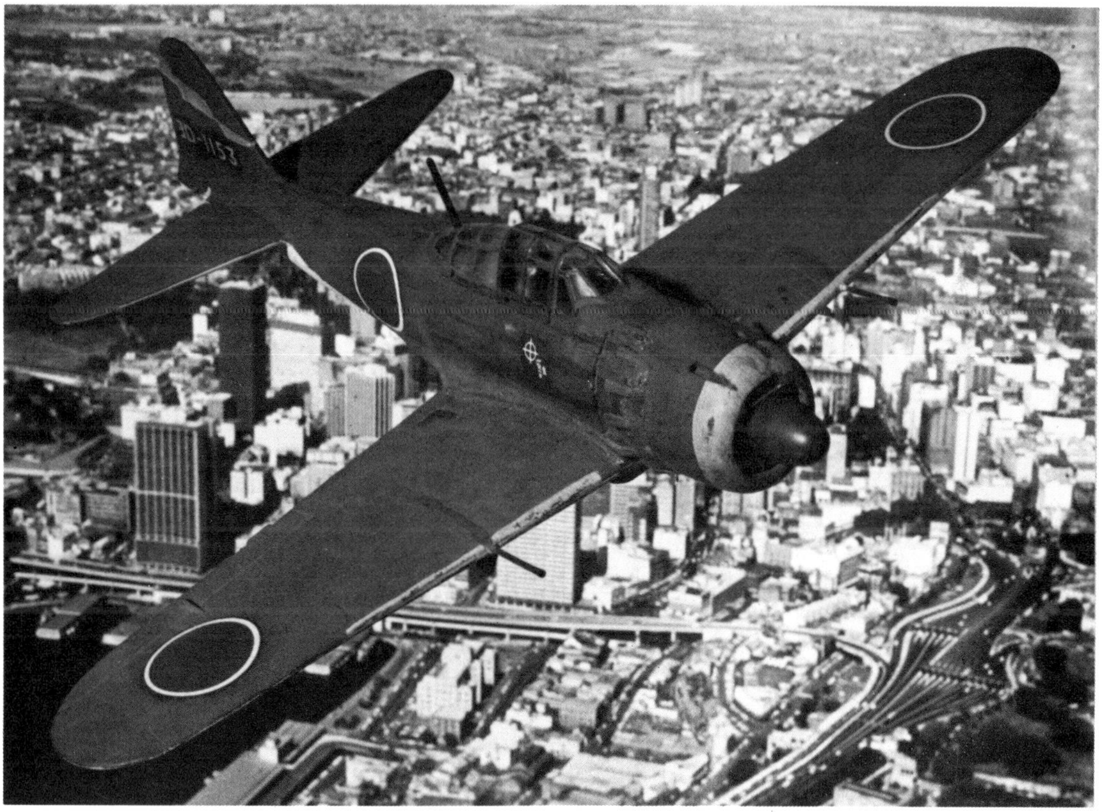

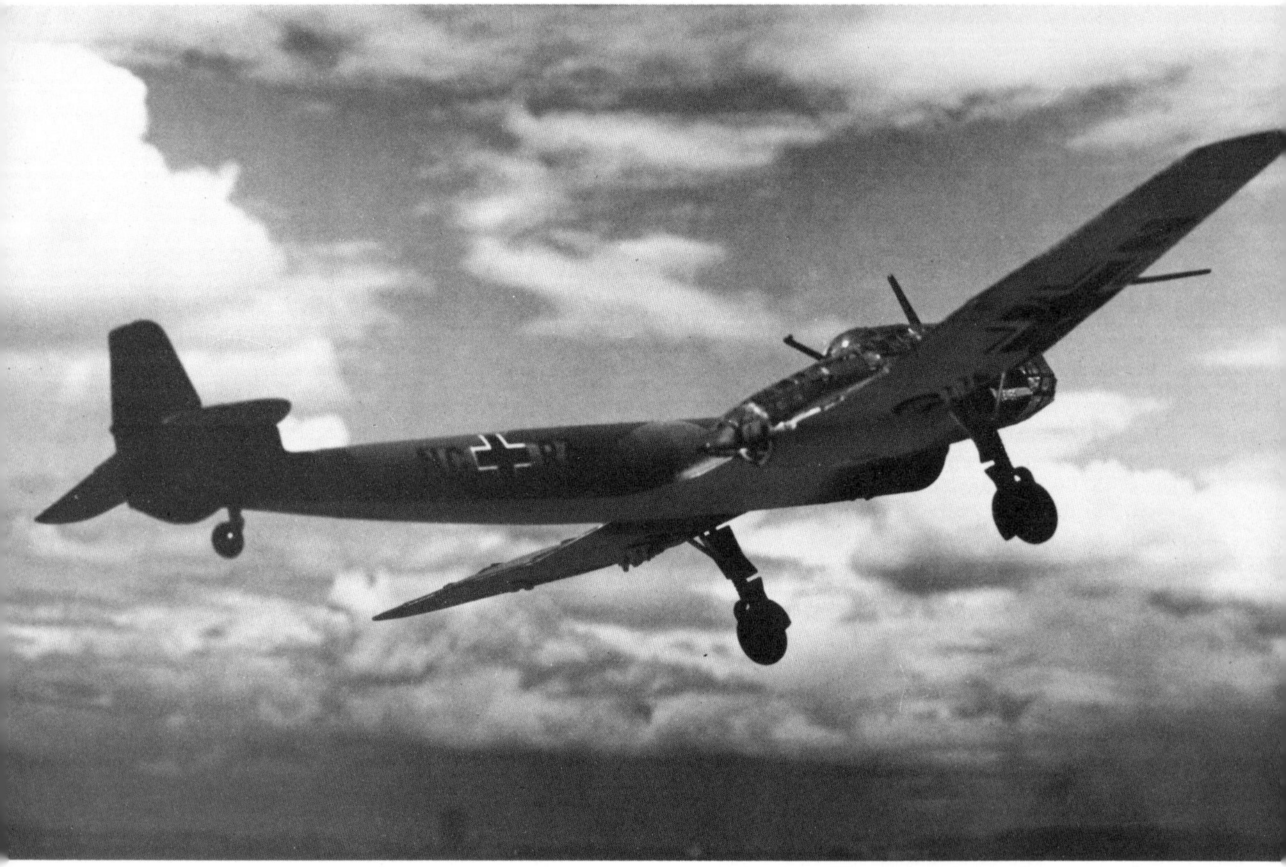

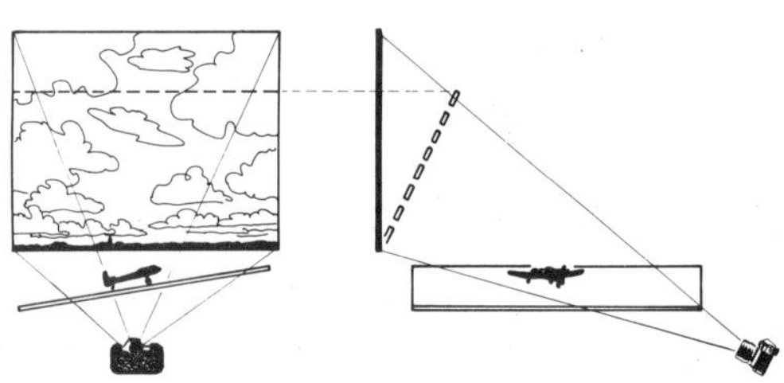

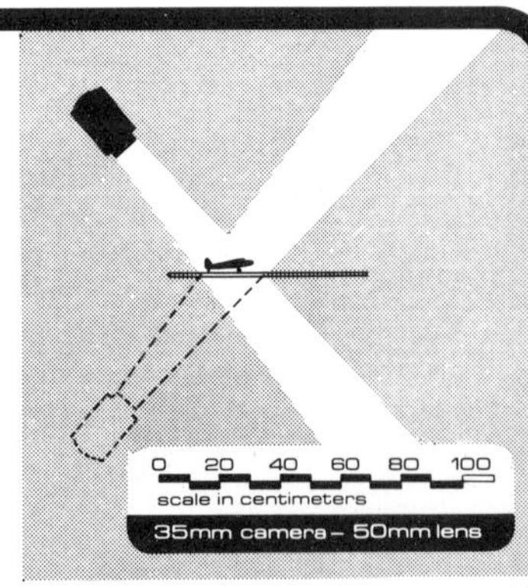

Another setting which had to be photographed from below the glassplate. Since all the three points on which the model rests are clearly visible, we had to tilt the glassplate in order to get the model in the attitude we wanted. Working through a glassplate, as shown here, is usually made difficult by the reflection of the spotlight off the top surface of the glass, onto the under-side of the model. (see inset).

J

J explains the occurence of the 'ghost' spotlight. There is not much we can do, except manoeuvre this light in such a way that the offending reflections miss the model's underside.

Figs. **61 - 63** differ only in angle; the impression of speed is achieved by pulling the ground over a distance of about 30mm during the exposure time (see diagram **H**).

Fig. **64** shows a photograph taken on the day a Fieseler Storch flew over Sydney. The set-up is relatively simple (diagram **I**A). This model was quite small and we could use a 135mm lens from only a modest distance to get the image to fill the entire negative. The Zero, on the other hand, being much larger, we took with the standard 50mm lens (fig. **65**). Notice how the use of different focal lengths in an otherwise similar setting results in various proportions between model and its background.

Finally an unusual problem in fig. **70**; we wanted to depict an aircraft immediately after take-off, climbing and banking away from the

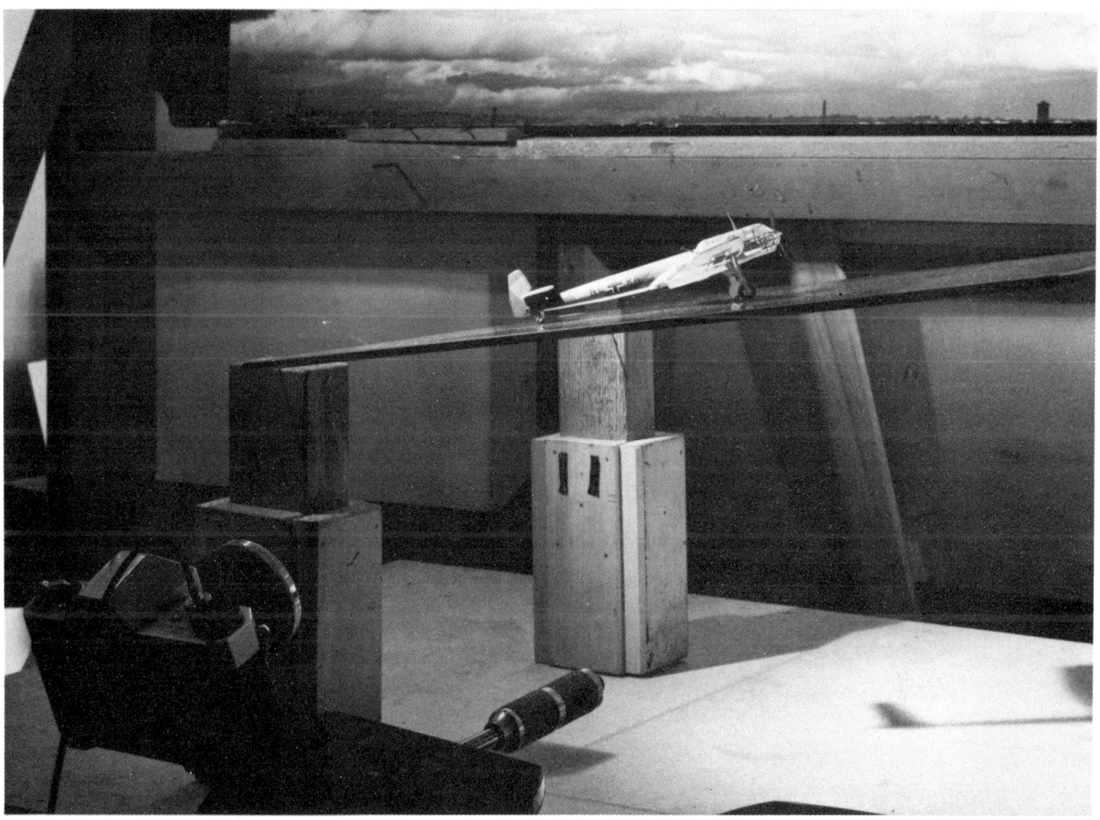

67⟩

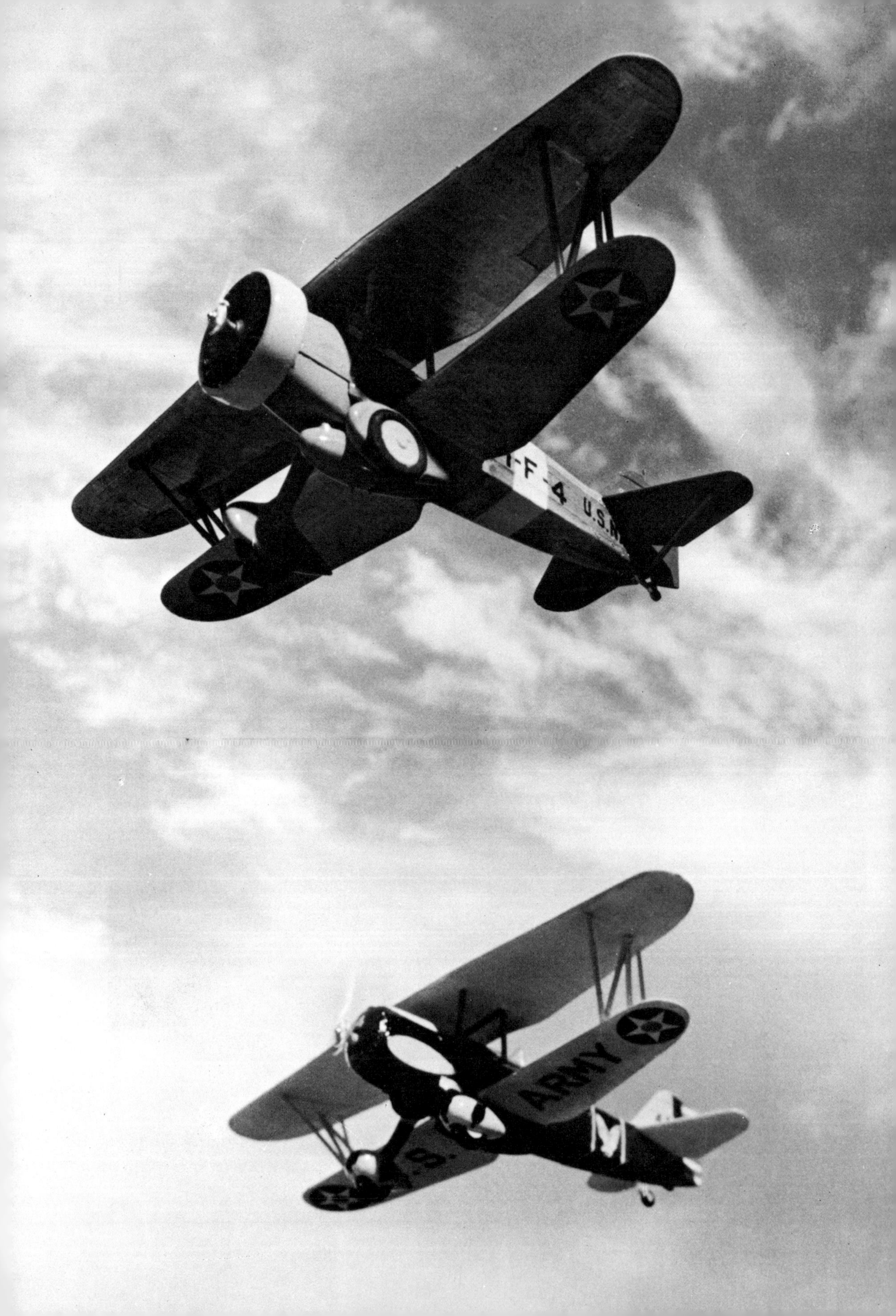
F-4
U.S.N
ARMY

runway. Diagram **J** supplies all the details, while fig. **67** is the actual set-up, just in case there are people still in doubt about the authenticity of the pictures in general.

The spectacle of two or more aircraft flying in formation is always a highlight in any airshow and it is only natural that we should try to capture two biplanes doing their thing. Before going into details we would like to examine the possibilities in this particular field.

In the first place there is the ground-to-air shot, which in real life of necessity has to be taken with a long tele-photo lens, simply because aircraft do not fly that low. As we have seen, pictures taken from a long distance are characterized by a certain flatness. In extreme cases this lack of depth (not to be confused with lack of depth of field), results in a totally unrealistic photograph. We have all seen films of horses in a race, taken from the other side of the track, coming directly towards the camera. The whole image is usually filled with horses and their jockeys, all galloping wildly. Yet they do not seem to get any nearer to us. These pictures are taken with lenses of up to 600mm, which on a 16mm camera is 24 times tele-effect. In these shots there is not much difference in the dimension of an object at the front of the scene, compared with that of a similar object at the back. If we take our photograph of two models with a short or even standard lens, the result will inevitably be that the far one appears much smaller than the near one, because we are close. Fig. **68** is an example of this, although in this instance the picture could have been taken from another aircraft flying below these two. The models used in this and the following shots were very small indeed, which presented us with a another unexpected problem: we could not blow the propellers, because blowing made the models fly off the set in the first place, as happened when we took the photograph for fig. **36**; secondly the little props did not build up enough momentum to keep on revolving during the whole of the exposure time and finally, the trick with the rod did not work, at least not with the models standing on their undercarriage. It turned out that the slightest pressure on the propeller not only made the prop move but the whole of the model with it. The difficulties were

A shows the relative position of our models in a horizontal sense; the arrow indicates the direction of our camera. B reveals how the models were propped up with small pieces of packing material. Both models and background inverted, photograph taken from above, as indicated by arrow.

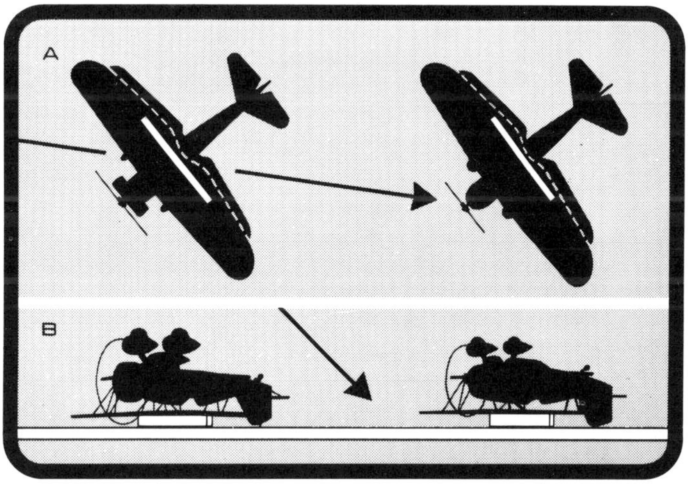

K

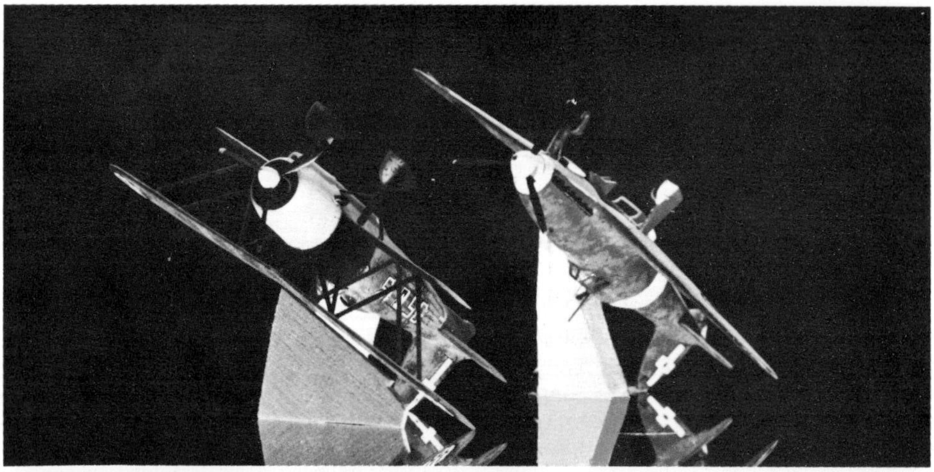

69

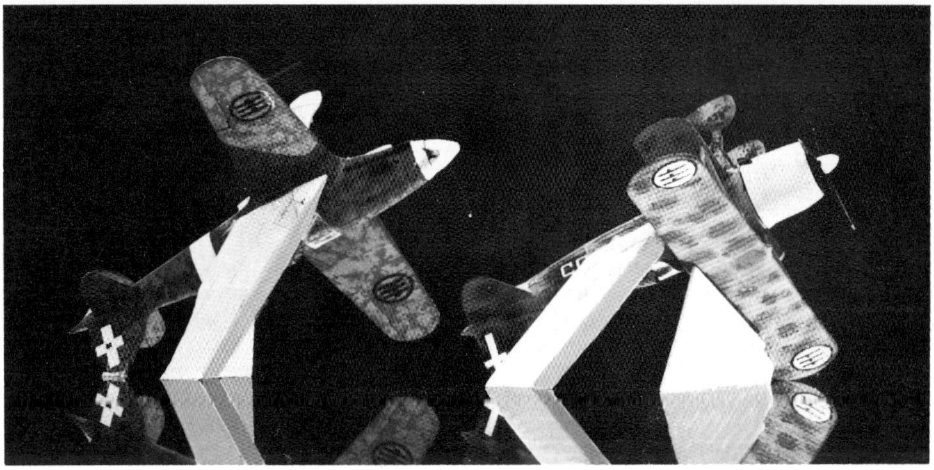

70

solved by again turned everything upside down and taping the models down on the glass plate, using small pieces of suitable packing material to bring them both in level flight. In fig. **68** the two aircraft are flying at the same altitude, in other words, they were taped down directly onto the glass without any further adjustments, other than the aforementioned packing under the wings (which was in reality taped on top of them!). See diagram **K**. Somehow we realized however, that this was not a realistic way for two aircraft to fly. One will always have to fly either below or above the other, quite apart from their relative position in the horizontal sense. The fact that these models were so small and consequently very light in weight, made it possible to position them as shown in figs. **69** and **70**, resulting in fig. **71**. The supporting structures must obviously be hidden entirely behind the models themselves,

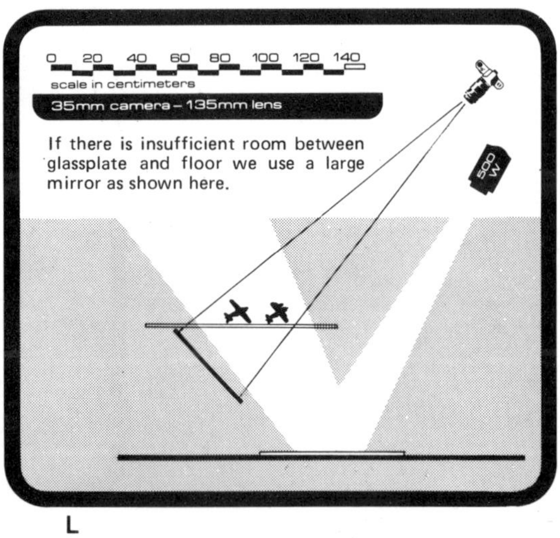

L

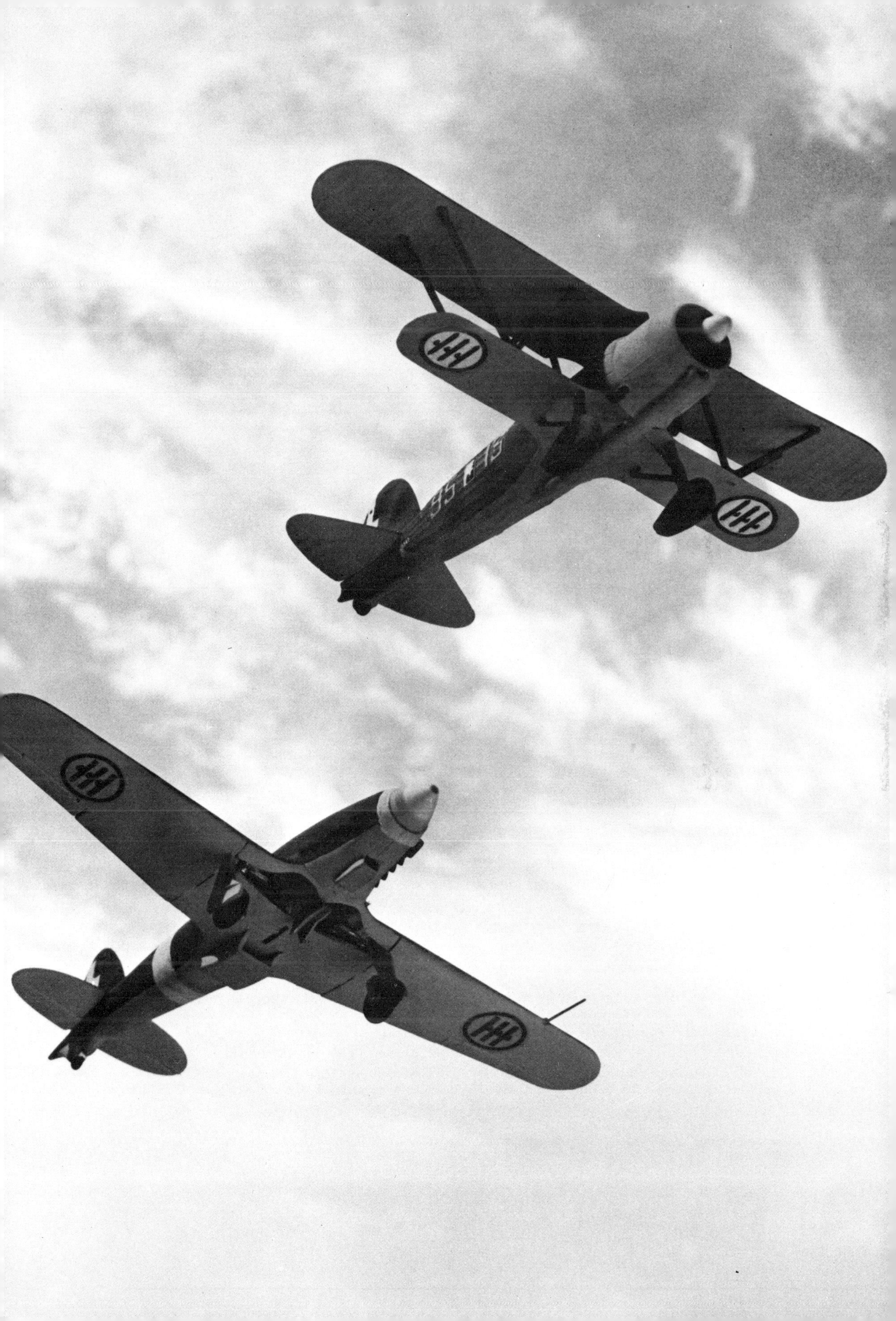

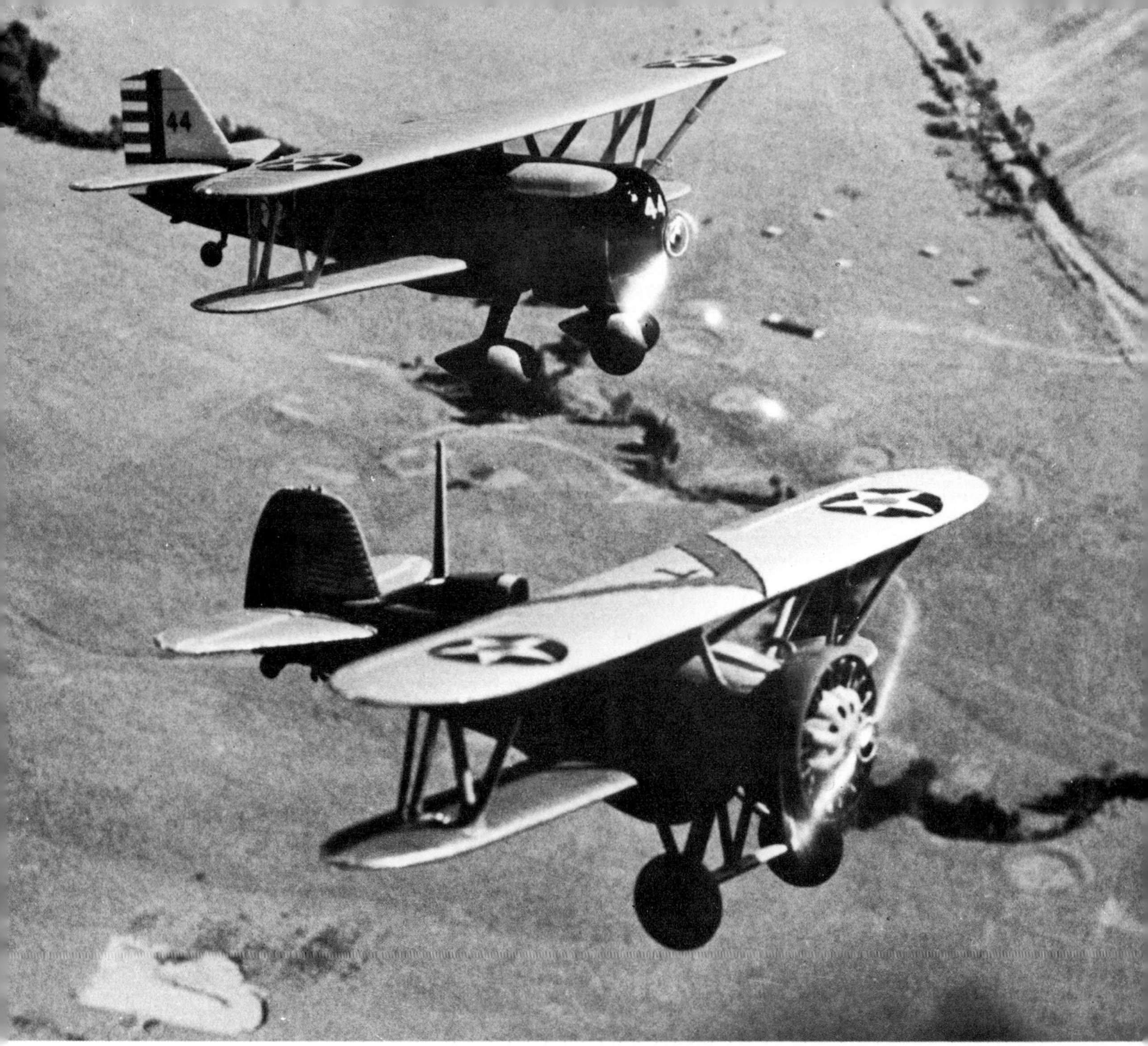

which created quite a few difficulties and we were moving the camera around for a considerable period of time before the proper position was found. Things were further complicated by the fact that we had decided to shoot this one with the 135mm lens. The camera was a fair way up in the air and we had to build the actual set as close to the ground as possible, which meant that there was not enough room for the spotlight. A large mirror solved our problems as shown in diagram L. The important thing is to position the two models in their proper relation; the Macchi Folgore had to fly below and behind the Fial Falco. Although the maximum speed of the Folgore is a clear 100 mph more than that of the biplane, they can fly together like this if the Falco puts in everything it can give; the Folgore had to lower its undercarriage to increase drag and so reduce speed. That, at least, sounds like a plausible explanation. The fact was, of course, that the undercarriage was fixed in that position and we had to use the model as it was. Take note that combinations like this have to be realistic. It may be nice to have a jet fighter beside a vintage biplane, but there it ends.

We need an assistant to turn the extra airscrew in these multiple-aircraft shots; it may require a lot of practising to get everything to operate smoothly. The two props will have to revolve together, although not necessarily at the same speed.

A relates in general terms to fig. 74; the arrow indicates that we find the horizon at A'; the model nearer the camera is consequently **flying lower** than the observer. B explains how in fig. 72 the horizon B' does not appear in the picture.
NOTE: Since aircraft do not necessarily fly straight and level, we have a considerable degree of freedom as far as the presumably "correct" position of the horizon is concerned. In fig. 72, for instance, our models are obviously flying a left banking turn.

M

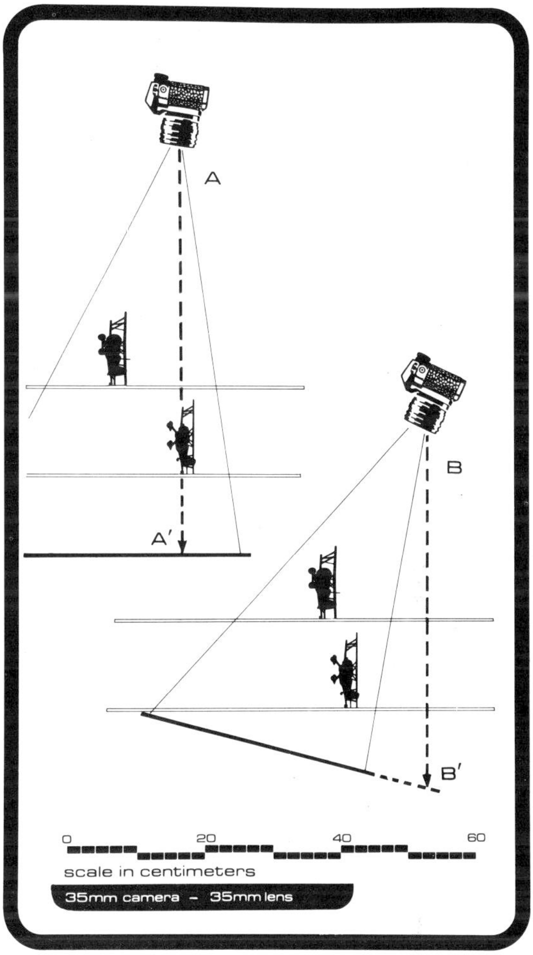

Fig. **72** shows an air-to-air photograph, the observer flying in the same formation. This effect was achieved by using two glass plates, one for each model, one placed below the other, as in diagram **M**, which supplies the details for both fig. **72** and **74**. Fig. **73** is the actual set-up. The reflections of the bright yellow wings can be clearly seen in this photograph, but as we explained earlier, they fall behind the model when seen from the position of the camera. Since the mainlight was on the side facing the camera, those parts of the aircraft facing the glass, were relatively dark and did not cause any disturbing reflections. In fig. **72** the sun was shining the other way and the shadows are on our side; however, the background was bright enough to be able to absorb most of the reflections. Also, we were not looking squarely at the glass and the polarisation filter had some effect, sufficient to reduce whatever was left to an acceptable level.

The shades may seem very dark in these photographs, but as the ground is far away and the sky (presumably) very blue, there is not much diffused light to brighten things up. The feeling of distance between object and background is however much stronger because a dark colour, and in our case, a dark tone, seems to come towards the observer, so contributing a little to the overall impression of depth and distance. Notice how in fig. **72** the starboard wheel seems to touch a row of trees; compare this with the same aircraft in fig. **74** against the haze of the horizon.

As in so many photographs, success depends on finding a compromise between what we want to achieve and the materials we have in hand: the first and most important condition is that our models are in focus. This demands the use of a short lens, because such a lens has a good depth of field. The background can be brought into good focus if we place it close to the models. So far we will have encountered few problems. The moment we switch on our spotlight, however, all this changes. We will find reflections and shadows of our models on the background. We can get rid of them by moving the light, which may result in a lighting we do not want, more reflections in the glass, or both. We can also lower the background, widening the gap between it and the bottom glass plate. This gives us more room to play with the 'sun', but makes it more difficult, if not impossible, to get everything in focus. On top of all these worries we may have a fairly small second glass plate, as we ourselves had. The shadows of the edges are quite capable of causing havoc in a carefully arranged set. The bigger the plates we use, the less likely it is that this will happen. Having balanced all the bits and pieces, positioned the lights in the best possible way and generally expecting to be ready to take THE picture, we may then find that we can not get our hand in between the two glass plates sufficiently close to

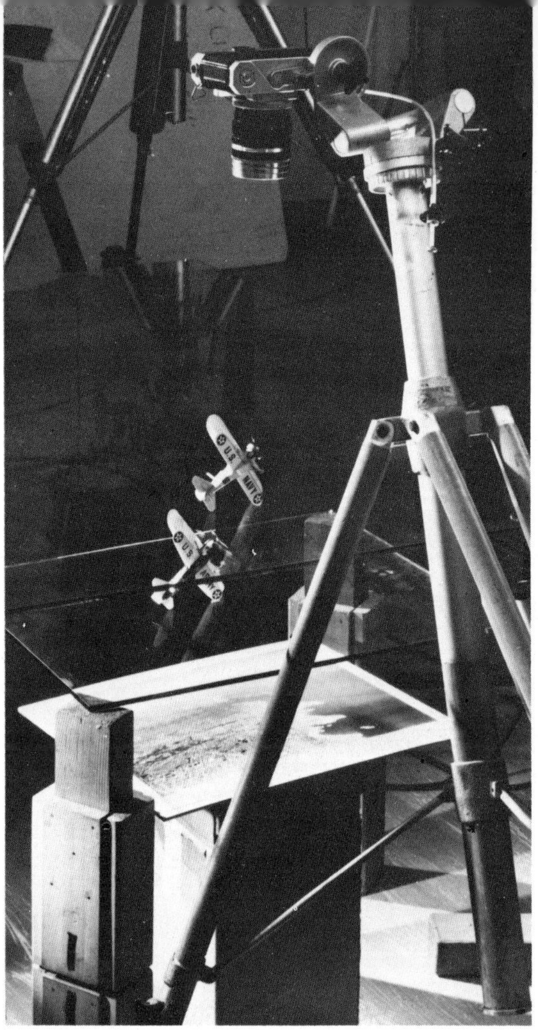

73

the propeller to turn it round in comfort; any rod longer than about 30cm will bend in a most alarming way, making it very difficult to control the prop properly. A large bottom glass plate will also hinder any adjustment of the model on it. Remember that we have taped the wingtips with narrow strips of transparent tape to the glass; in most cases the bottom wing requires a small piece of packing to bring both models in alignment. Since all this will of necessity have to be invisible, we can only use the smallest quantities of either tape or timber (usually balsa) and it is surprisingly easy to upset a delicately balanced model. So there we have an argument for a smaller glass plate, as well as for a larger one. We know that the two plates will have to be reasonably close together and we also know how this can cause trouble. We would like to place our background directly behind our models, to avoid losing any of its detail, only to find ourselves in the greatest difficulties with unwanted shadows. Perhaps the challenge of having to bring all these factors under control, explains why we went through three whole rolls of 36 exposures before we were satisfied with the photograph in fig. **74**. We mentioned most of the stumbling blocks we may meet while we were busying ourselves setting the whole thing up, but there are others, and they only become apparent after a film has been developed. Our rod, activating the prop of the far aircraft, was too dark in our first effort (which extended, of course, over a complete 36 exposure film); we made it lighter, to match the background better, we thought, and then it turned out to be too light. That we found out after another whole film. In the end our rod was painted in two tones, half of it a lightish grey, nearer the model, and the other half of it a darker grey where it went across the darker sea. The correct tone is extremely difficult to assess: in the first place, wet grey paint is a good deal lighter than dry grey paint; in the second place, wet paint is very reflective, even if it is matt. A newly painted rod will therefore shine as if it was just polished, which in turn makes it quite impossible to tell the final tone of it. In a setting as critical as this, it also becomes important on which point in space we focus our lens. In this instance (fig. **74**) the actual focussing point was located 50cm from the back of the camera; this gave a slightly lesser definition in the nearest aircraft, but superior sharpness in the second one and in the background. We could have focussed on the first aircraft, because the nearest focussing distance on this particular lens is 40cm. Stopping down, however, did not increase the depth of field sufficiently to give an acceptable definition in the background. Remember that stopping down also means an increased depth of field towards the camera, and by selecting our point of prime focus on the nearest object, we lose the advantage of this. Unfortunately this can not be observed in the camera: a fully closed lens darkens the image in the viewfinder to the extent that you may as well be looking in the dark. Again, as we have found so many times before, experience is our best teacher.

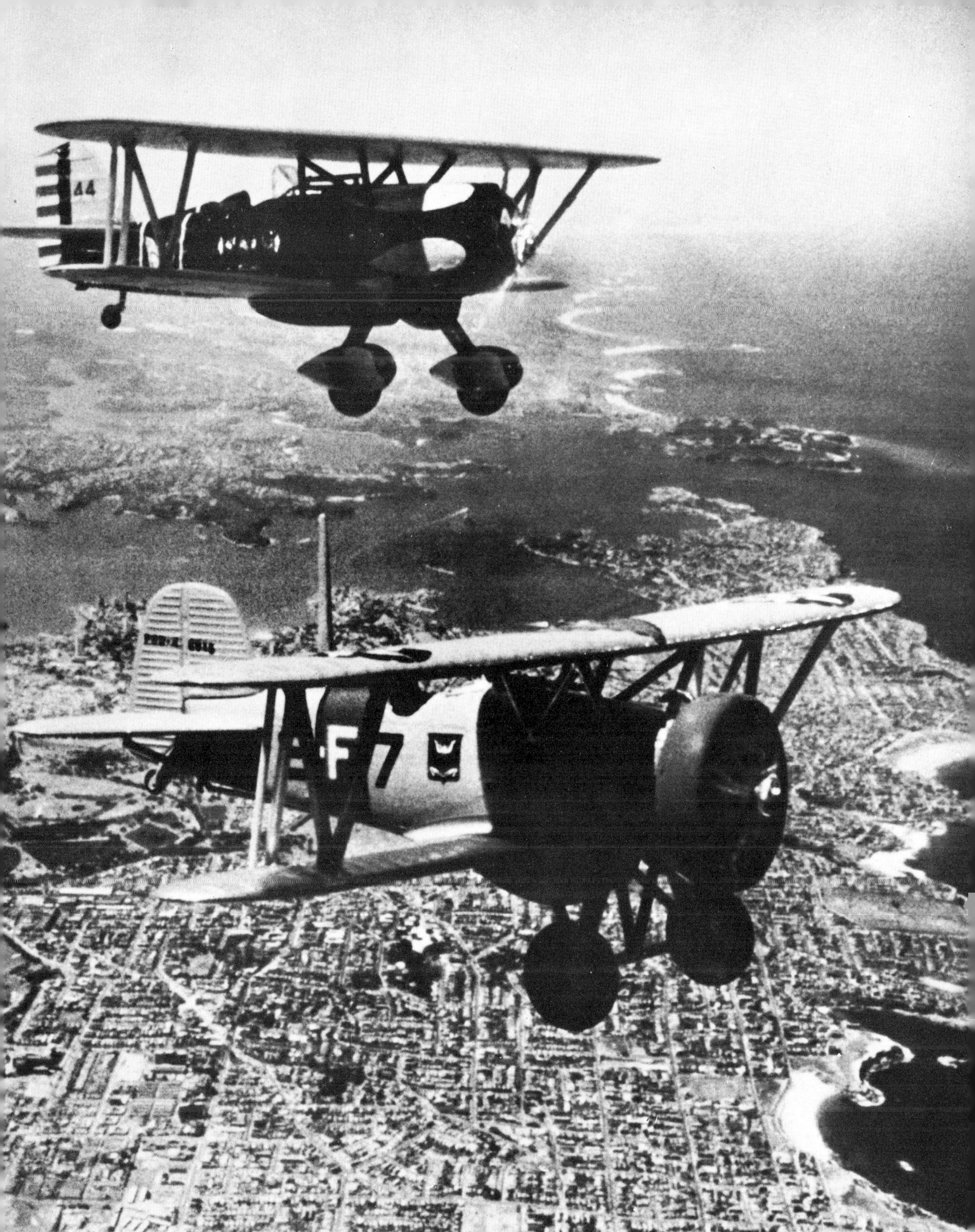

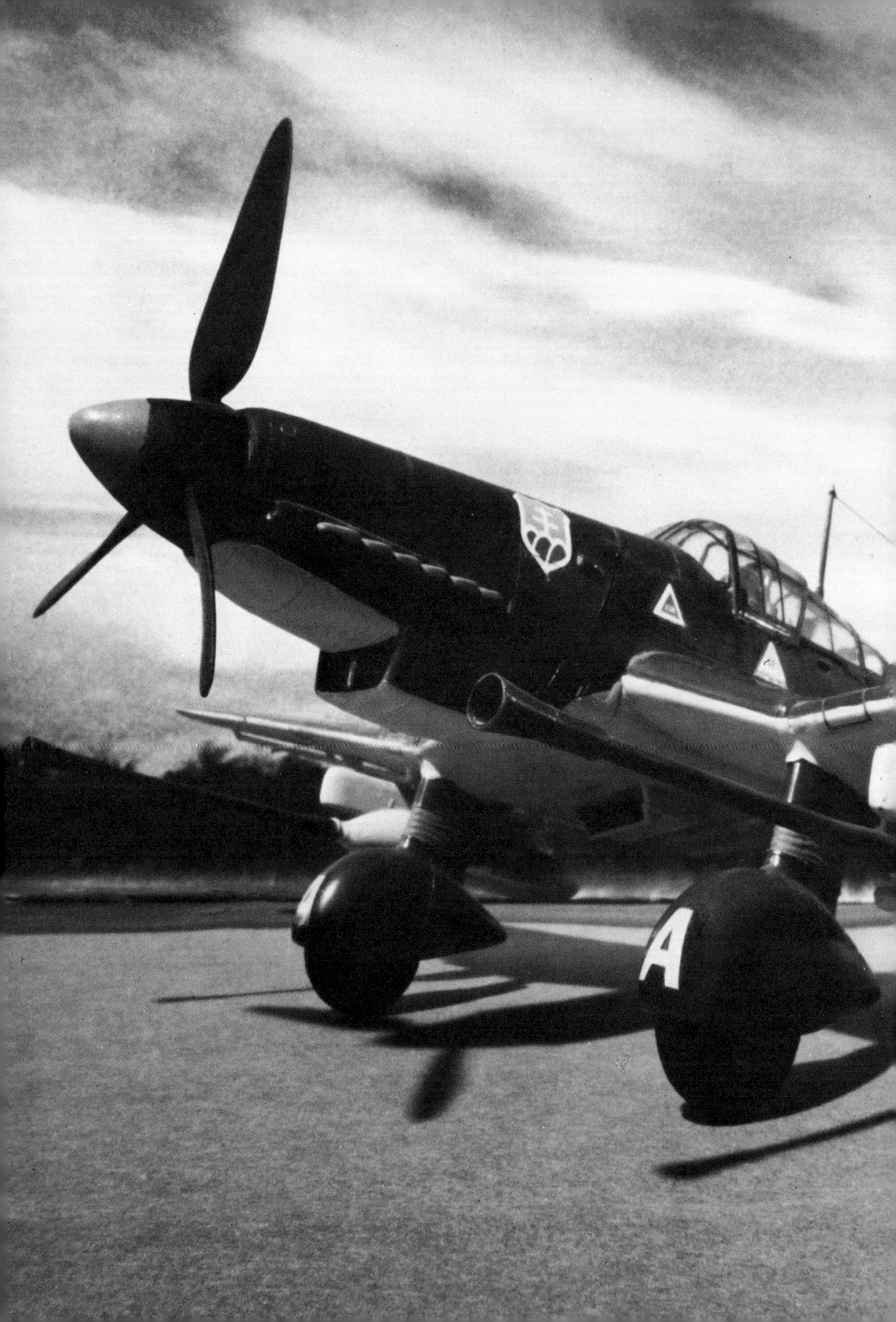
A

CHAPTER

7 EXTREME CLOSE-UPS

In this last chapter we shall see, amongst other things, what we can do with special equipment. This is possibly well out of reach of the average amateur photographer, but the topic will be, we hope, of interest to many. Professional photographers are rarely satisfied with the available camera when it comes to doing something which is not strictly conventional. All photographs presented here so far, are not really unconventional by present-day standards. It is indeed doubtful whether it would be possible to take such photographs of such fairly orthodox objects that scale models are. For a photograph to be un-orthodox these days, it would have be a long way out indeed. Anyway, the principle of photography itself hasn't changed since it all began, has it? There is absolutely nothing wrong with producing good, old-fashioned pictures.

Whenever we had to photograph a small architectural model, we realized how little we could achieve with the available equipment, and we began to think about building something more useful. No camera on the market today, will focus to approximately 3cm without the help of extension tubes or close up lenses; nor is there one in existence that produces the full image-circle on the negative and so enables the user to select exactly that portion of his negative he wants to print. Every lens produces this full circle, of course, but the camera manufacturer has decided for us which part of it we are to use, by building in the film gate.

Bearing all this in mind, we built a camera that had a very wide angle lens, in this case 100°. Since the whole of the image-circle appears on the negative, not one single degree of this is lost when we focus on something very near. The circle merely becomes bigger and bigger, just as in an ordinary camera, but there the gate remains the same and so the field of view becomes narrower. The optical system in our special camera has a focal length of 21mm and it can be stopped down to f/22. Somehow we managed to mount this lens, together with the shutter of an otherwise unserviceable WWII aerial camera in and around the focussing mechanism of a very old lens, way back from the days when lenses were built with multi-grooved focussing rings, which allows our lens to travel back and forward the best part of 20mm.

Armed with this camera, which is incidentally of the view-type, we are indeed able to do things we could not possibly do before. Fig. **75** is a good example of this: we focussed on the muzzle of the nearest 30mm anti-tank cannon, and stopped down to f/22. It is indeed a very welcome property of short lenses that they have such an extreme depth of field.

The distance from the lens to the muzzle of the gun was about 50mm, yet the whole scene is in reasonably good focus. Almost the entire aircraft appeared on the negative, except for part of the port wing, which was really more behind the camera than in front.

We have to be careful when printing these wide-angle shots: ultra-wide angle pictures often give the mistaken impression of being distorted. A distortion, however, is a condition found in lenses that have been badly designed, or in ones that have been damaged and are out of alignment. What these photographs are suffering from is extreme perspective, which is something the eye never sees. As we have discussed, we are unable to take in the whole scene and we have to look from one point to another. This is further complicated by the fact that our retina is curved. What we would see if it were suddenly possible to see everything in one glance, would certainly be quite different from what we have become used to seeing in photographs. In a camera the image is formed on a flat surface and straight lines remain straight. In photographs taken with a wide-angle lens of, say 100°, the perspective can play very strange tricks, especially near the edges of the image. Great care is therefore called for, not only when printing, but also when taking the picture.

Our model in this and the following shots

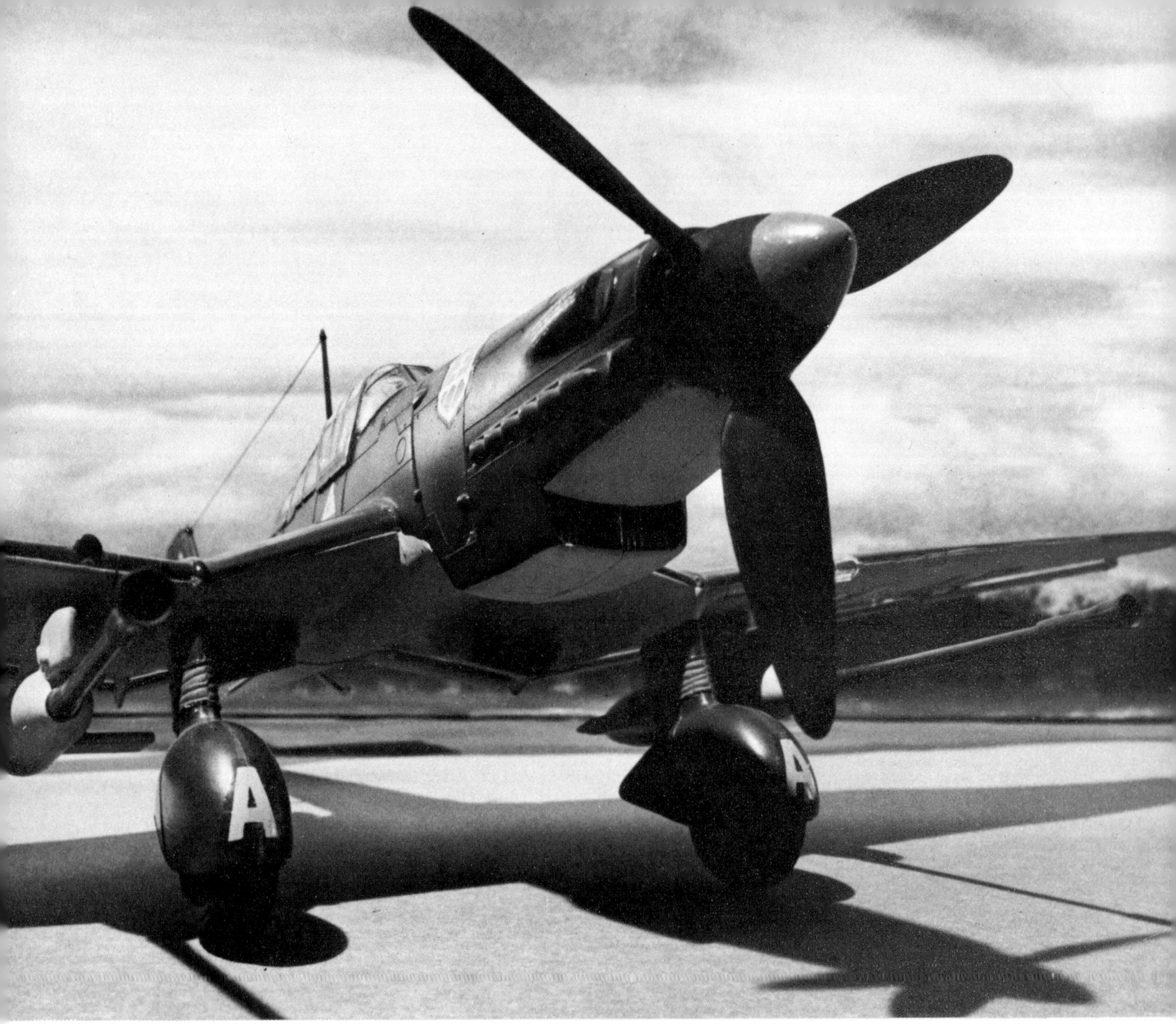

76

(figs. **75-84**) is a $1/48^{th}$ scale Junkers Ju 87-G with a wingspan of roughly 30cm, which makes it a very comfortable model to work with. A bigger one would demand a larger background, while a smaller one would inevitably suffer from a lack of fine detail, or, alternatively, an abundance of too coarse detail.

The 'wide-angle syndrome', as we might call it, shows again in fig. **76**, accentuated by an enormous airscrew. The reasons for fig. **77** were two fold: we wanted to prove that a propeller could be safely worked with a rod while being almost on top of the camera and we wanted to balance the general composition of the photograph by rendering the propeller invisible.

We will now give some further thought to the burning question of where the horizon ought to be in photographs of this nature. On page 40 we quoted a rule, the essence of which was that the horizon is always the same height above the ground as the centre of our lens; diagram **N** (page 71), although related to fig. **81**, illustrates the principle. We can either work on a reliable three-view drawing or carry out the survey on the actual model. If we make sure that the optical axis and the horizon are the same height above the ground, we should have no worries. In figs. **76** and **77** the horizon is approximately 10mm below the average height of the tree tops. Unless we have an unlimited expanse of airfield behind our model, the skyline will always be above the horizon.

These photographs can undoubtedly be improved by adding more detail to the ground; we used a plain grey sheet of cartridge paper, darkened in parts, to suggest the verge of a runway, but otherwise left bare. A carefully

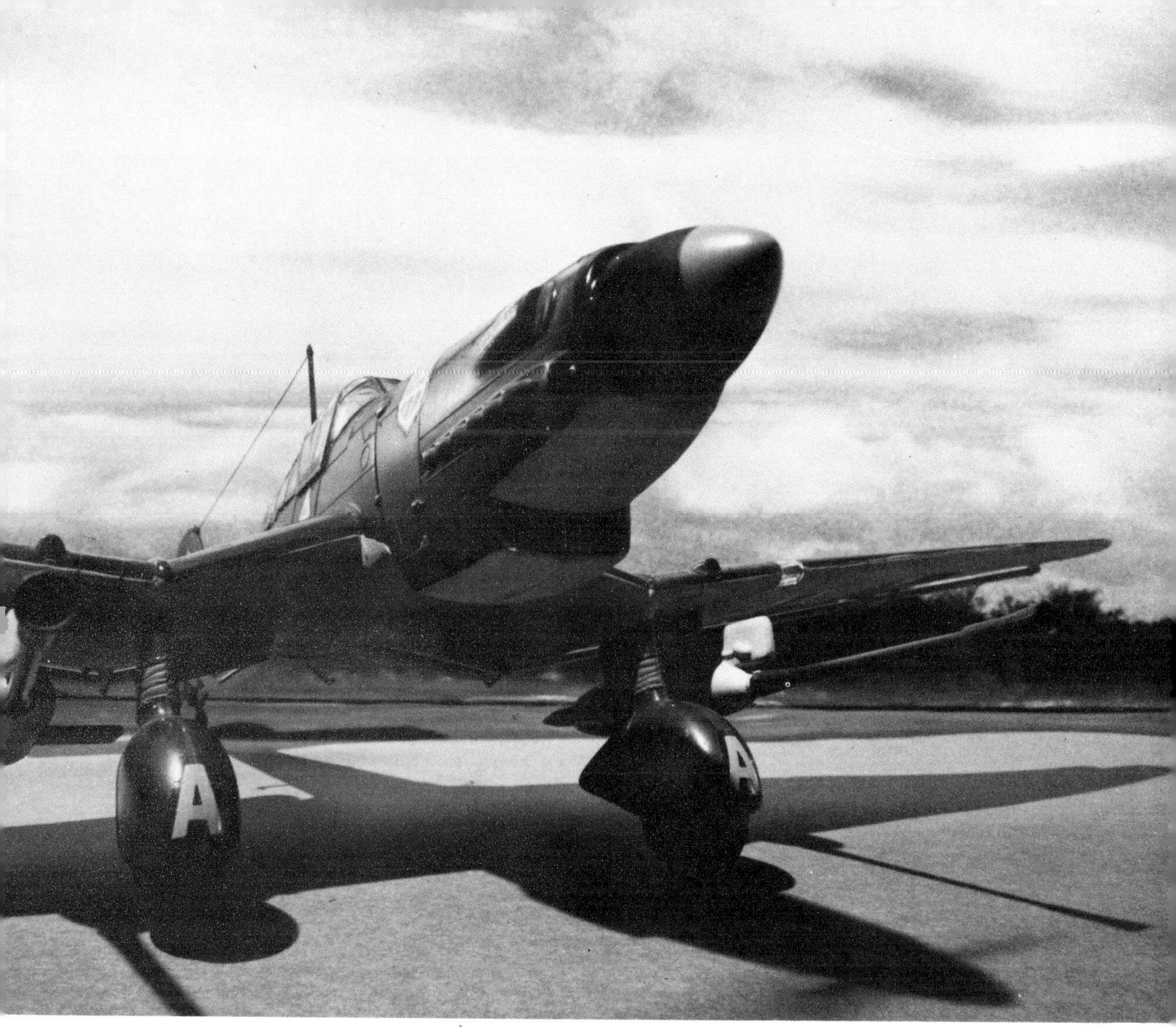

77

drawn concrete slab pattern, complete with cracks and oil stains, would add tremendous realism.

Fig. **78** is exactly the same setting; however here we have tried to introduce some 'atmosphere' by lowering the sun to almost horizontal and by darkening the sky except for a narrow strip just above the trees. This was done by shading the required section of the background during the entire exposure.

Photographs of combat aircraft, taken during active service are very seldom, if ever, 'beautiful' in a photographic sense. More often than not we will find that pictures taken in the air were blurred, due to high air speeds, and possibly due to the fact that not all airmen were photographers. In our studios we are working under ideal circumstances and we can produce attractive pictures. Just how unrealistic these are because of that, we have not been able to determine as yet. Maybe our models are more glamourous than their full-sized counterparts. This is particularly true for photographs from a bygone era, such as WWI. Film in those days was not only orthochromatic, it was also very susceptible to haloing. In many a ground-to-air shot the aircraft was nearly washed out by halo from the white sky; blue sky was never recorded on film then.

One distinctly annoying thing about our models, specially noticeable in these close-ups, are the wheels, the tyres of which invariable give the impression of being inflated to some 1,000 lb per sq. in. If they would only settle a little under the weight of the aircraft our pictures would be so much better.

It is not always possible to fill the whole negative with our model, nor is this indeed always necessary. We will examine how sensible

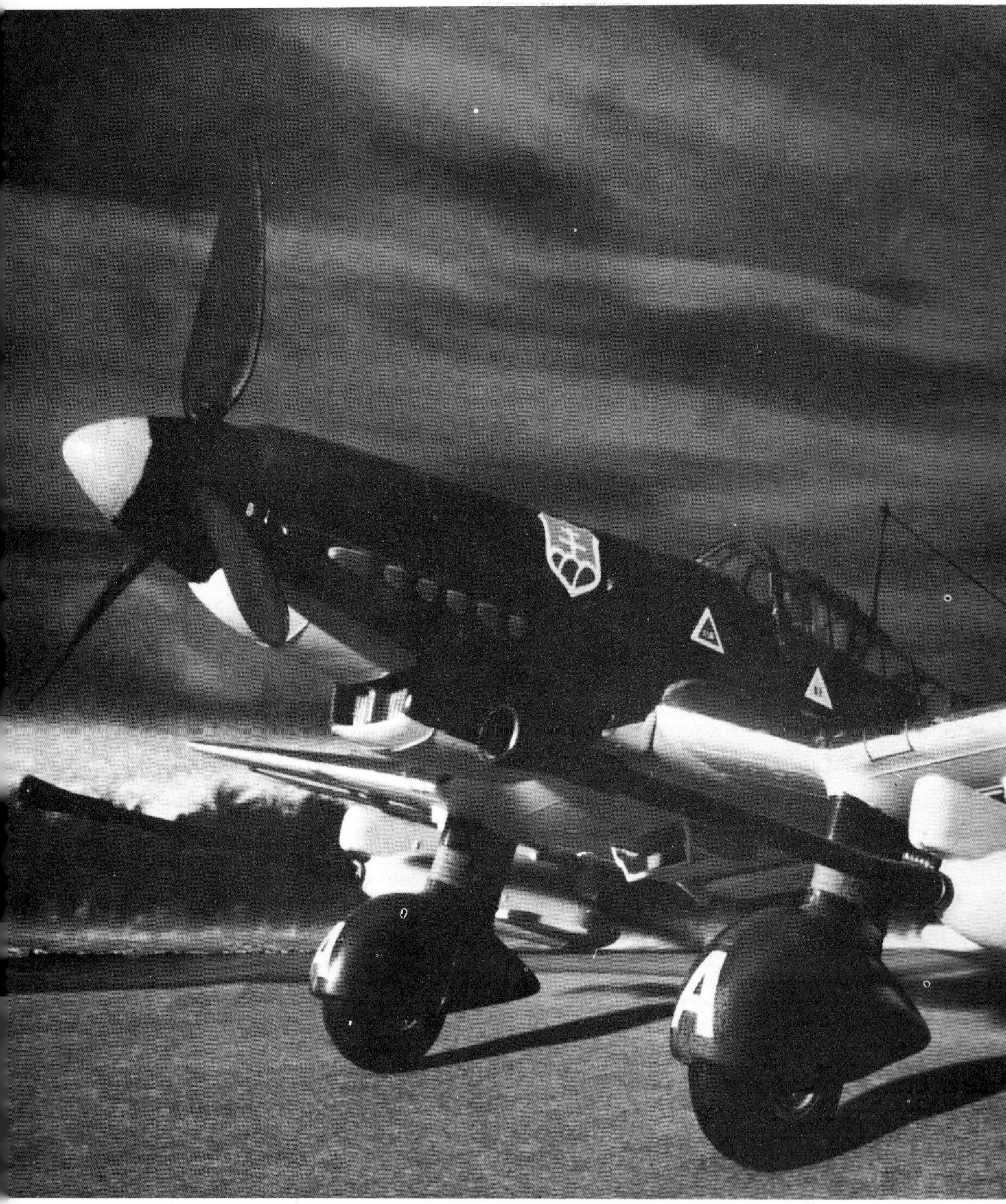

78

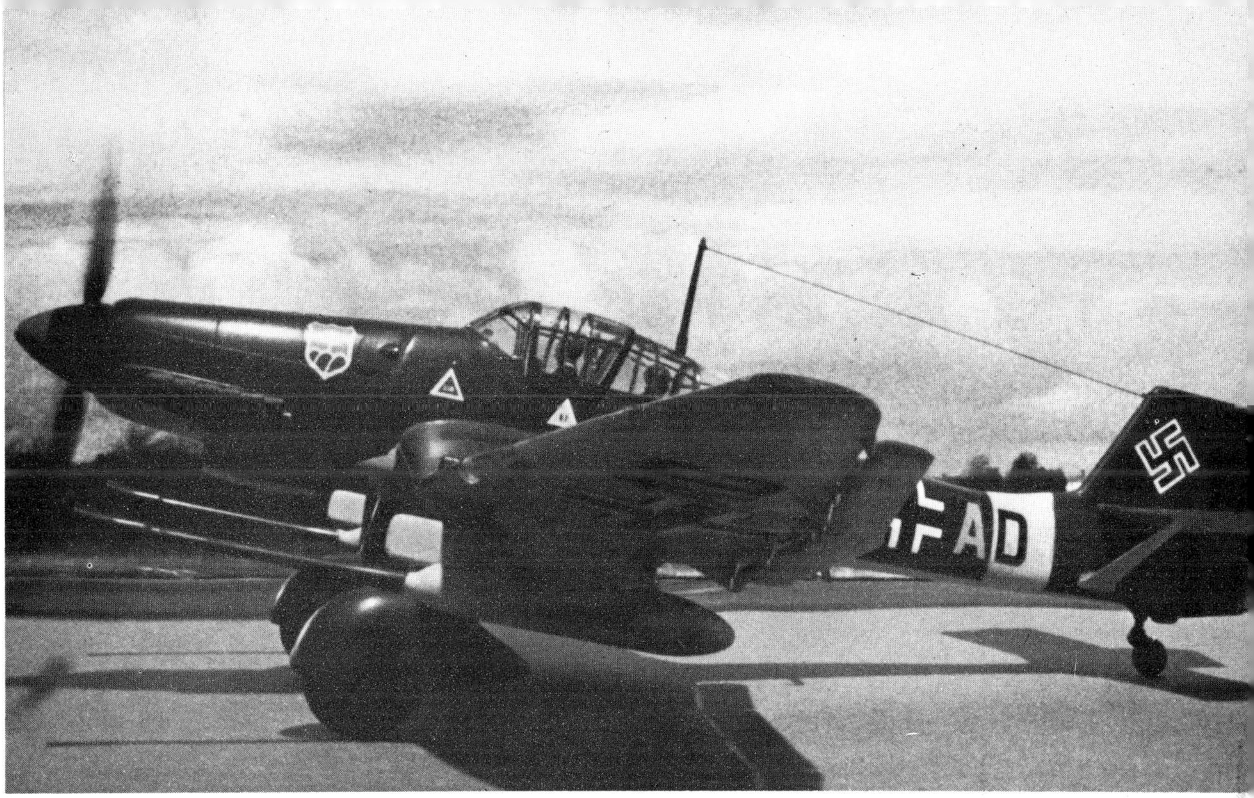

trimming or cropping of a negative produces a better picture than just printing the whole of it would do. Wide-angle lenses are apt to include more of our object than we, strictly speaking, need: this is certainly so for our special camera with the 100° lens. We consider it an advantage however, for the simple reason that it is better to have too much of a certain thing and be able to crop, than not to have enough of it. We warned against exaggerated perspective; these are the pictures where one could easily become entangled in unrealistically stretched wings. We mentioned also that we had to be careful when taking very-wide angle shots. A few examples will throw some light on that rather vague statement, we hope.

Fig. **79** is taken with the ultra-wide angle, but from an increased distance. We had to crop the negative drastically and the result is of course a picture that could have been taken with a standard lens. The advantage, however, is a very good definition in the background, due to the good depth-of-field properties of the very short lens. Fig. **80** is a contact print of the actual negative, on which we indicated the cropping.

It is extremely difficult to give rules that would help to avoid eccentricities such as occurred in figs. **81-84** Perhaps the best course of action is to take the photographs without worrying too much about this and straighten things out in the darkroom. It is however an undeniable fact, that certain angles do not result in outrageous pictures. A good example of this is a wide-angle shot of a flat wall; we assume that we are looking straight at it, and the resulting photograph will be a simple elevation of that wall, without any perspective and consequently without anything to indicate that this was a wide-angle effort. Our models are never flat, so we can not expect this to happen. Moreover, we do not want to photograph our models flat. The

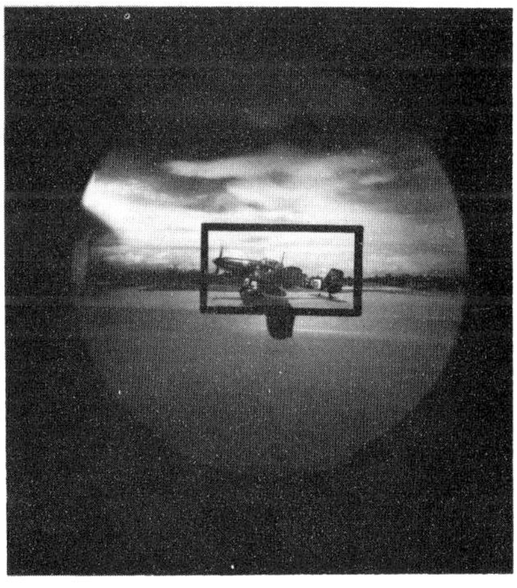

80

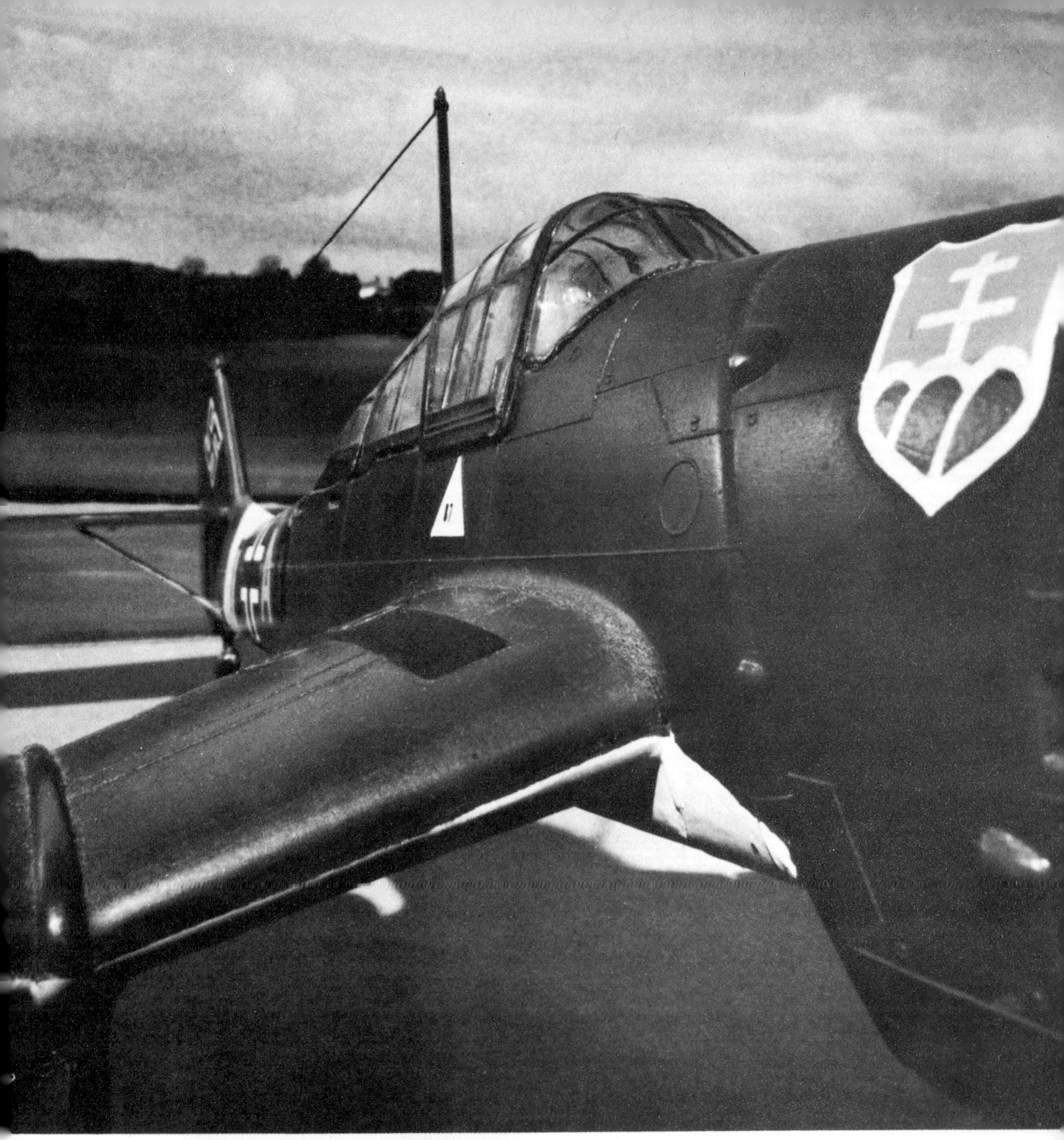

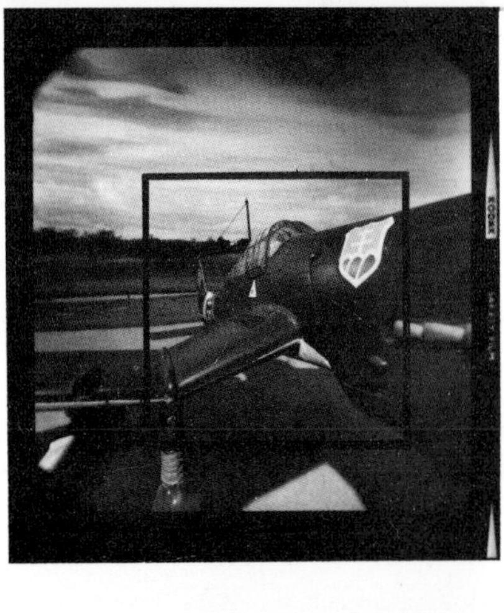

82

more directly towards the camera a part of our object extends (such as a wing), the more we will experience this exaggerated perspective, as in fig. **81** on the extreme right-hand side of the picture, and in fig. **84**, where it happened at the bottom. Still, we feel that the overall presentation of our model in fig. **84** is more acceptable than fig. **81**. This explains why the cropping was less severe. Notice how a positive loss of angle occurs when this camera is focussed

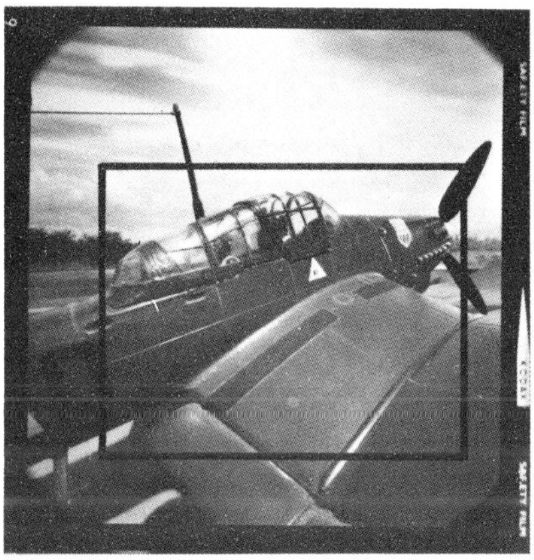

83

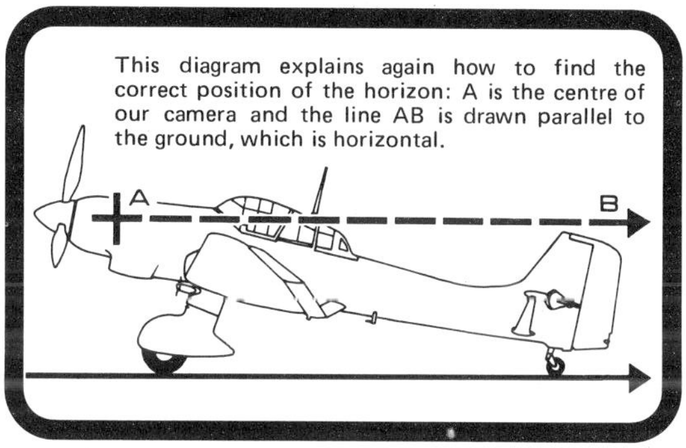

N

This diagram explains again how to find the correct position of the horizon: A is the centre of our camera and the line AB is drawn parallel to the ground, which is horizontal.

at its closest range, which is approximately 50mm. This contradicts an earlier statement, where we claimed that this would never happen. However, up to a distance of 75mm the image circle fits nicely within the frame of 55 x 55mm.

The foregoing applies only to very short lenses, which are readily available for 35mm cameras; owners of 35mm lenses, which are the ones most commonly found, do not have to be unduly concerned. For those with lenses of 24mm or 28mm, however, the dangers are very real.

We have reached the end of the seemingly endless string of aircraft in fig. **85**, which shows the interior of a Spitfire, built to 1/9 scale. No special tricks in this shot, just the by now very

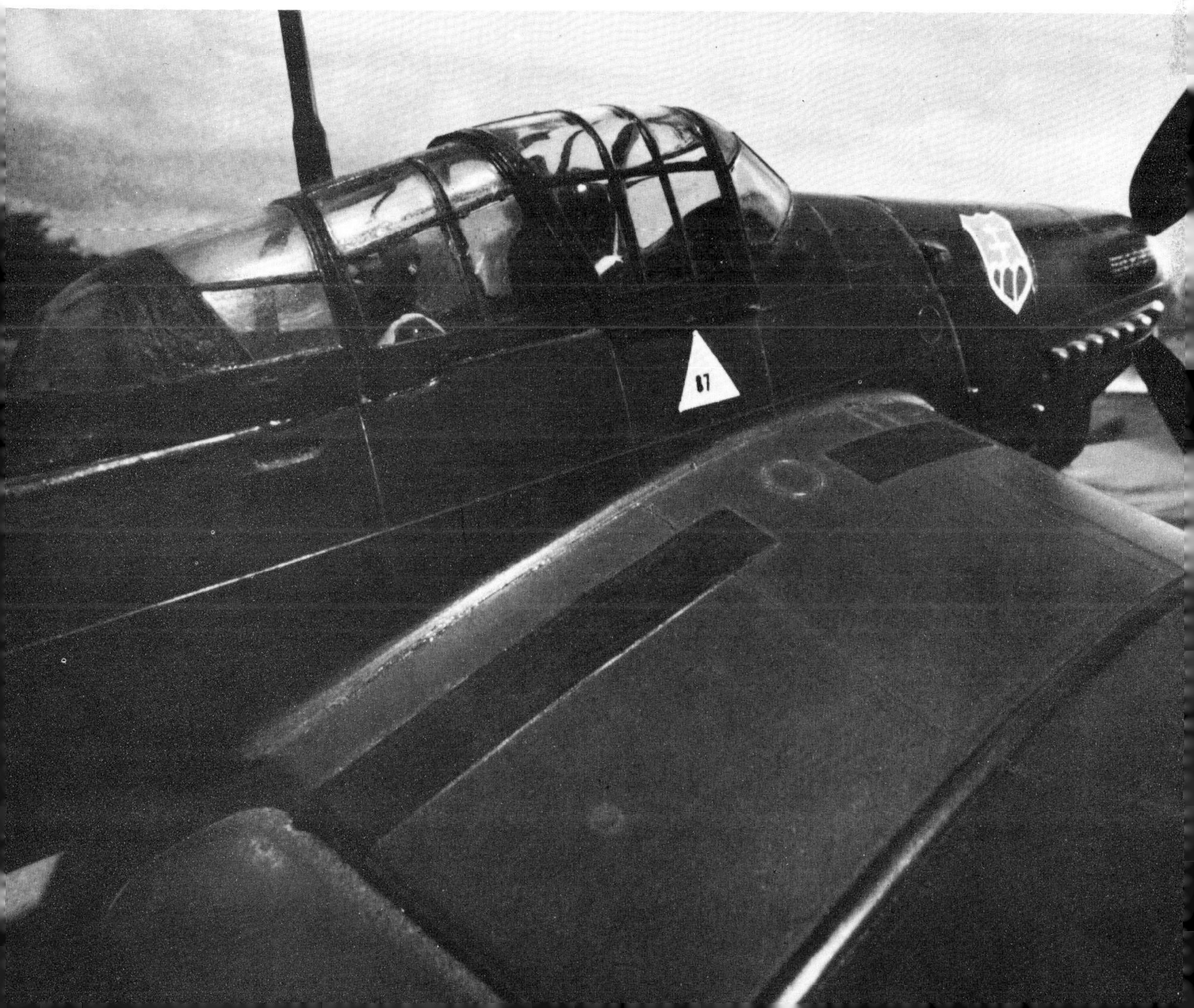

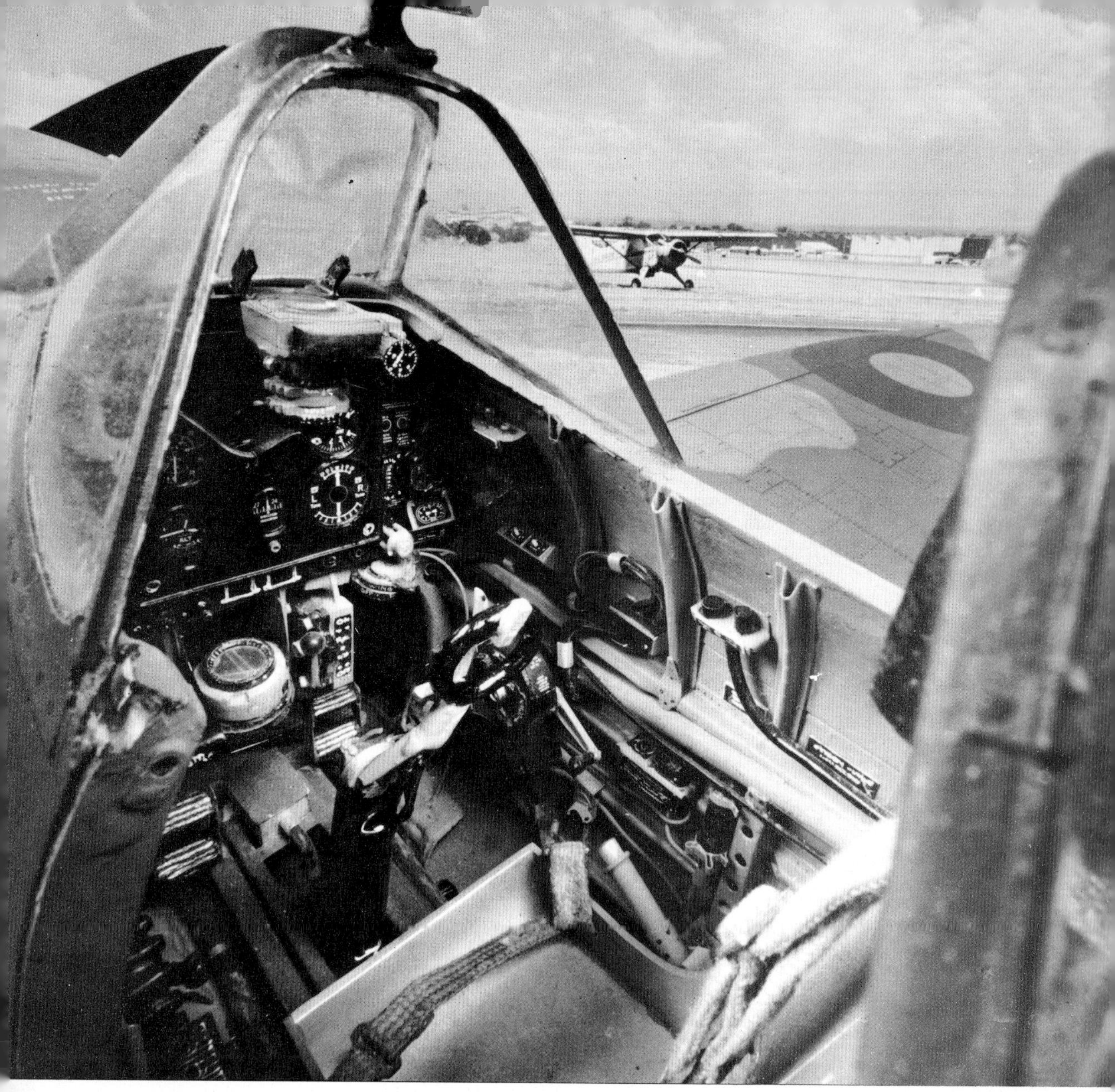

familiar background. We didn't even have to worry about the ground because the starboard wing took care of all that. The space inside the model, though fairly large by model standards, is not particularly big photographically speaking, and it proved a bit tricky to get enough light inside the cockpit. Getting it full of spotlight would have been easy enough, but it was impossible to fill-in the resulting shadows to an adequate level. We therefore used a different kind of illumination altogether: a bank of eight 65W fluorescent lights, suspended directly above the model. The result is probably much better lit than the inside of the real Spitfire ever was.

This photograph once again makes us realise how important it is to put the observer's eye in a spot where it would normally be if he were looking at the real thing. If we can succeed in doing just that, we will have won half the battle.

All attempts to take photographs of ships in real water were soon abandoned; the nature of water is such, that whenever we tried to make it behave the way we wanted, the results were without exception disappointing and a more convincing solution had to be found. To sum up the many shortcomings of the average dish of water: it is too shiny; it is far too transparent, unless we mix it with paint or ink to give more substance; its surface is too flat and the waves, if there are any, are totally out of scale; the ripples it does produce are travelling far too fast, which makes it impossible to freeze any waves we may have succeeded in forming. Surely we can find something better to do with this water than letting it make a mess of our photographs as well as the inside of our models.

Thinking along these lines, it seemed obvious that blown-up photographs of suitable waves would provide the answer to this problem, and so we found ourselves with cameras and all aboard a pretty small fishing cruiser amidst 3 meter-plus

O

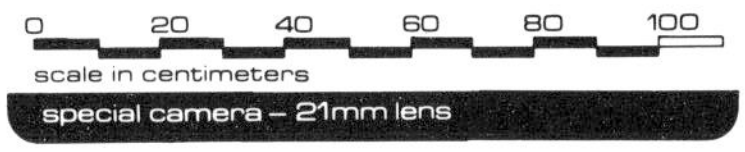

In this setting the background consists of two parts: A is a print of sky, which has to include at least the horizon at its lowest part, and stretches far enough upward to allow a substantial portion of our model to be photographed against it. B is a print of waves, cut out and mounted as described in diagram P. These two are then positioned in such a way that the top of the waves just cover the horizon of A. This method allows us to use a photograph of sky taken on dry land, provided always that no tall trees or other objects not normally found at sea, protrude any distance above our horizon. With the model as close to the background as this, we have to be very careful with shadows. Note again the position of the horizon H in relation to the camera.

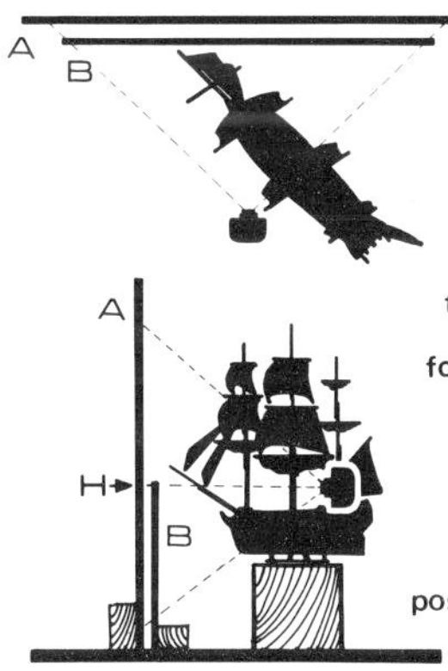

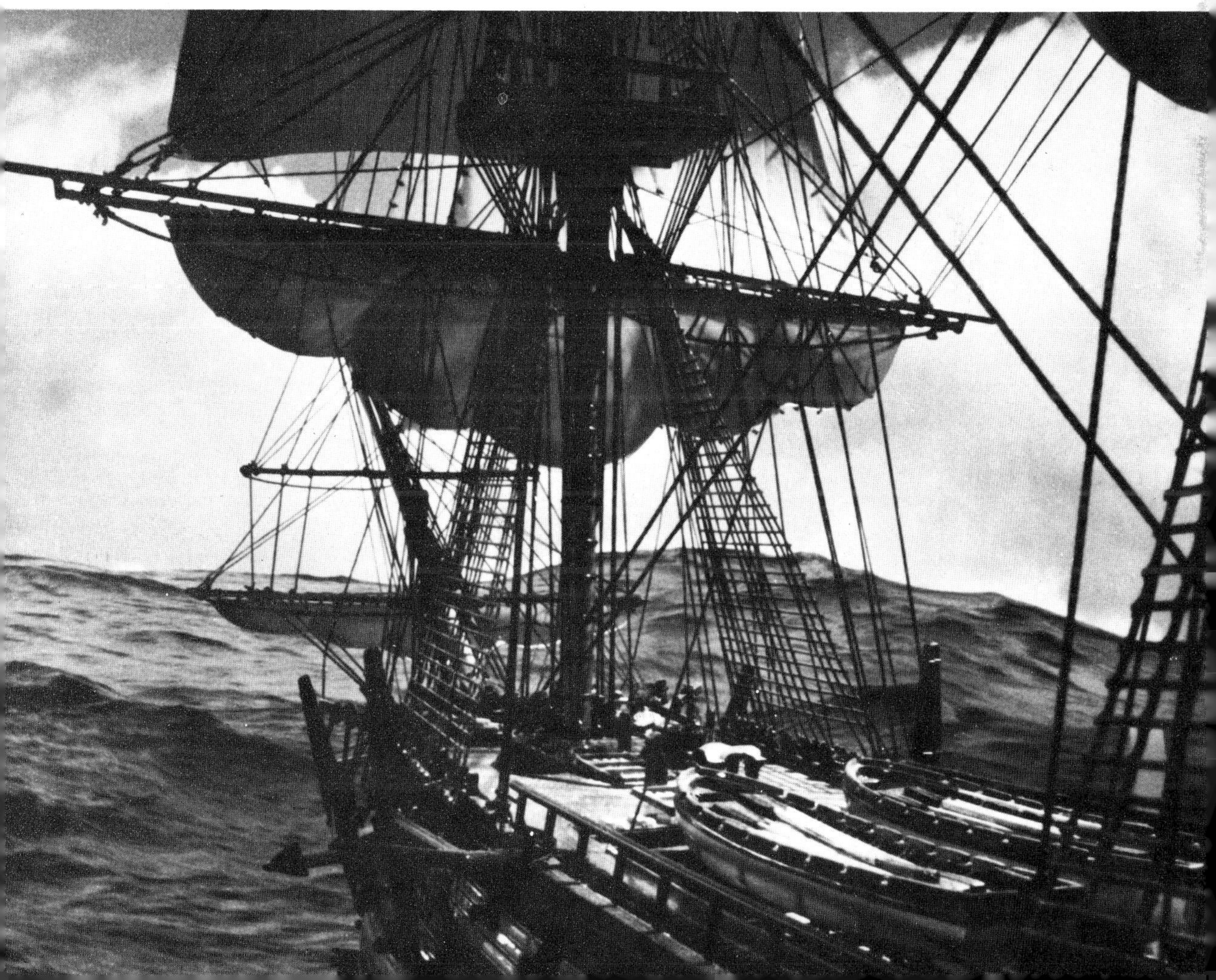

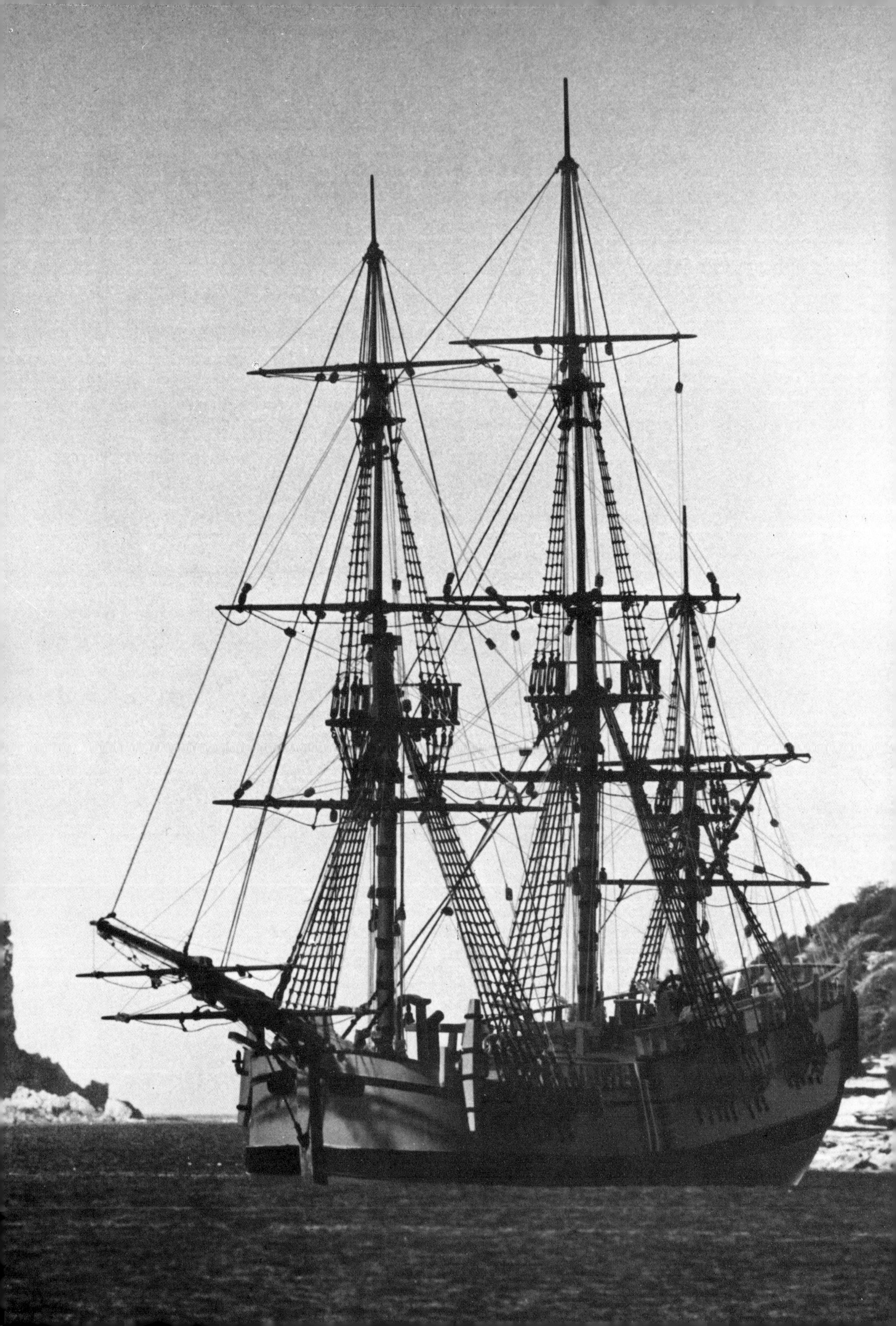

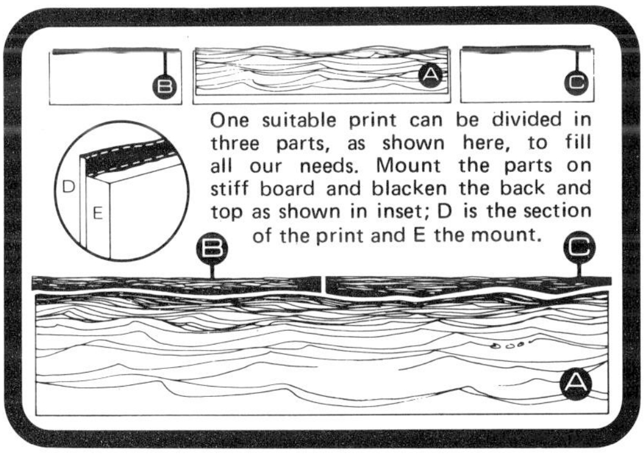

One suitable print can be divided in three parts, as shown here, to fill all our needs. Mount the parts on stiff board and blacken the back and top as shown in inset; D is the section of the print and E the mount.

P

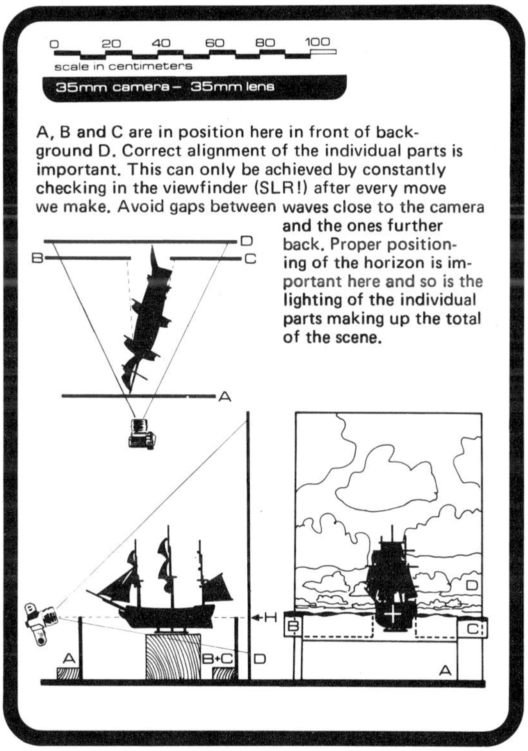

A, B and C are in position here in front of background D. Correct alignment of the individual parts is important. This can only be achieved by constantly checking in the viewfinder (SLR!) after every move we make. Avoid gaps between waves close to the camera and the ones further back. Proper positioning of the horizon is important here and so is the lighting of the individual parts making up the total of the scene.

Q

waves one very windy, and seemingly never-ending day. By the time we had resumed our normal complexion, the films were developed and dry and we knew it had not been in vain. After carefully selecting a few of the most spectacular waves, we enlarged these to suit the model. Of course we harvested only waves; getting these and an interesting sky as well would have been a miracle indeed. We already had more than enough suitable clouds, and the two had to be separated anyway to be of any use in the kind of setting we were going to build; this involved the fairly elaborate process of cutting along clearly defined lines, as shown in diagram **P**, and mounting them on board to make them stand up properly. The top edges of these prints must be painted black, because the strong light coming from above (our main light) will illuminate the top much more than the side facing the camera, and, as the paper in section is pure white, this top edge will seem to light up, resulting in a wave with an extremely artificial-looking bright line all along the top.

Another point to watch, is that whenever we use photographs in our backgrounds, we must make sure to place them in the set the same way as we took the photograph of it. This may sound confusing, but it is in fact quite simple, once the principle is understood. If we take a picture of, for argument's sake, a street scene, to be used in a setting with models of cars, then this photograph will show this street in perspective. If we now re-photograph the completed scene with this background in any other position than parallel with the film-plane, then we will introduce another perspective, superimposed over the one already there. The result will be a terrible mess. We do not have to be too fussy about this alignment, however, since an angle of a few degrees will not produce any perceptible distortion. Alternatively, if we have decided to paint part of the scenery, such as for instance a road or a landing strip, which is to be placed horizontally and on which we are going to put our model, then we have to draw this without any perspective whatsoever. Where we are using a combination of these two systems, which will be in the vast majority of cases, and which will take the form of a vertically placed background. horizontally placed ground, the background will have all the perspective, while the ground has none. It is of course difficult to describe the perspective of a plain, cloudless sky, but as soon as there are a few clouds, we will see them becoming smaller and smaller towards the horizon. All we can see of them there, is a more or less straight base-line. This is a distinct feature of clouds near the horizon and we must take great care to make sure we do indeed have this type of cloud there,

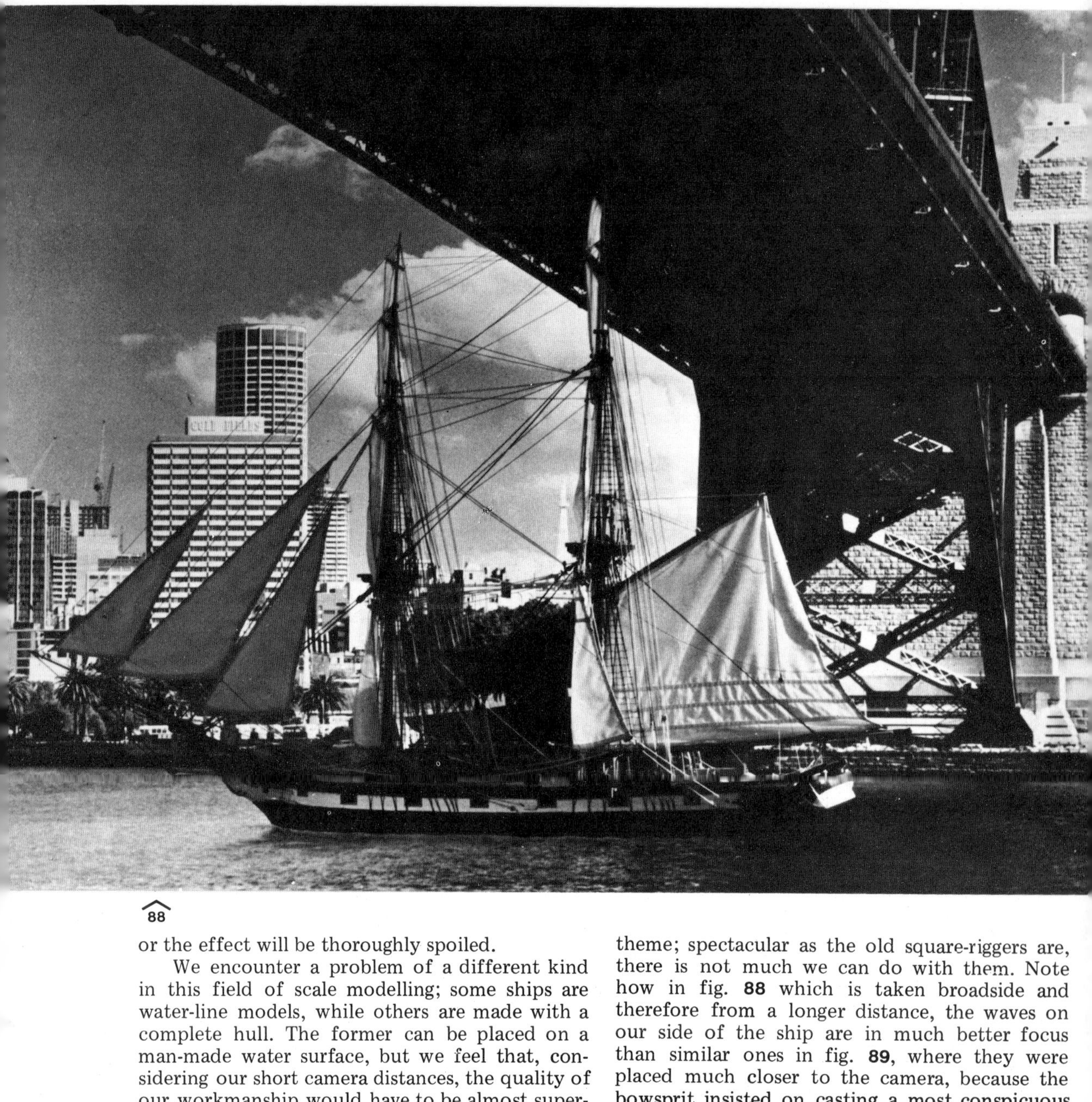

88

or the effect will be thoroughly spoiled.

We encounter a problem of a different kind in this field of scale modelling; some ships are water-line models, while others are made with a complete hull. The former can be placed on a man-made water surface, but we feel that, considering our short camera distances, the quality of our workmanship would have to be almost superhuman to achieve the same results a properly executed photographic set-up will yield.

Fig. **86** is a good illustration of the freedom we have when we try to put the observer's eye in a likely place: the only possible way to see things this way, would be dangling from a yard-arm!

Figs. **87-89** are merely variations on the theme; spectacular as the old square-riggers are, there is not much we can do with them. Note how in fig. **88** which is taken broadside and therefore from a longer distance, the waves on our side of the ship are in much better focus than similar ones in fig. **89**, where they were placed much closer to the camera, because the bowsprit insisted on casting a most conspicuous shadow on them. This model of HMS Victory, was unfortunately suffering from rather old age at the time these photographs were taken. The effect of the constantly changing humidity in the atmosphere on the rigging and the thin plastic parts to which this is attached, can be clearly seen. In this last photograph, some trouble was caused by light reflecting off clouds on the right

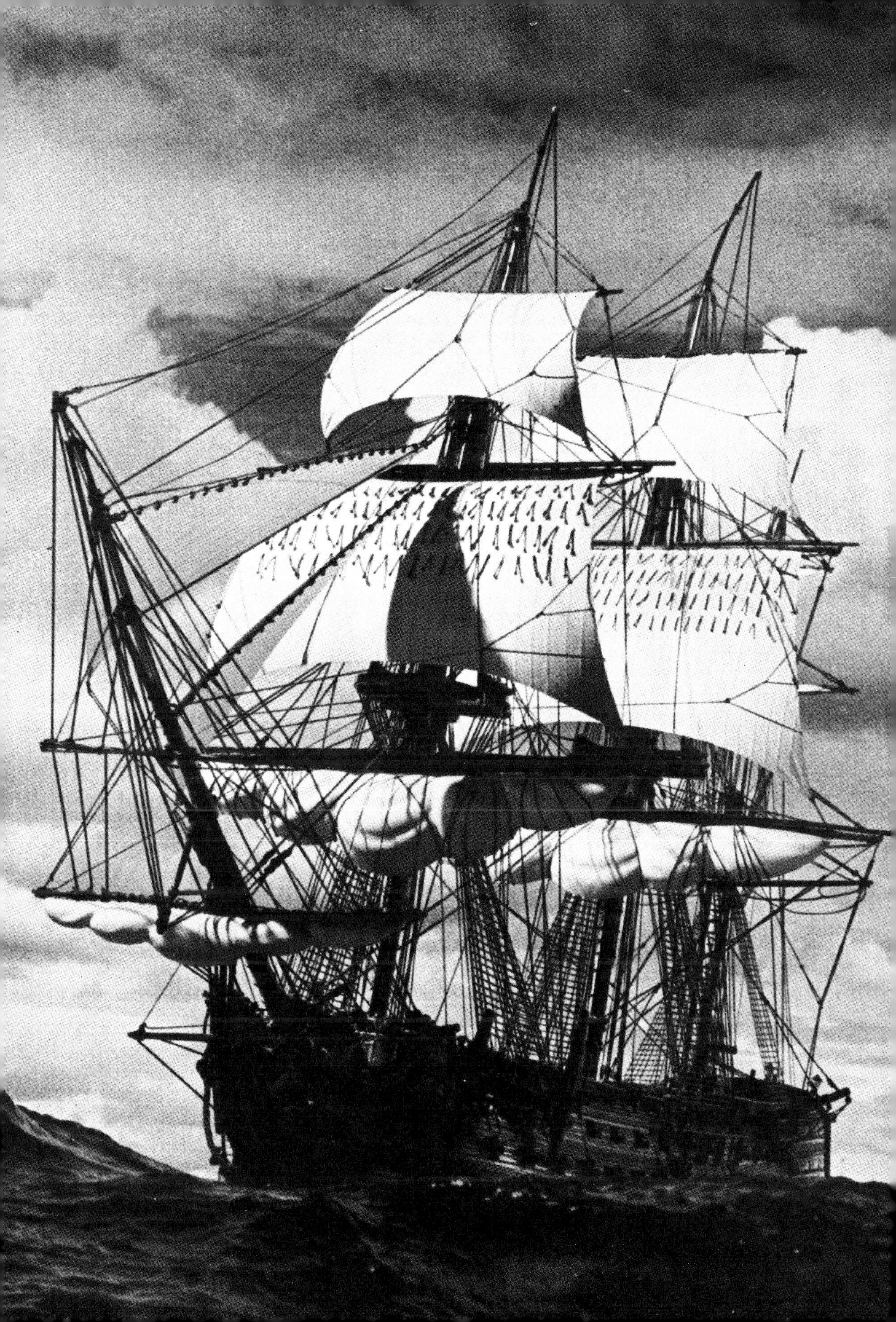

hand side, not even appearing in the picture, illuminating the port side of the hull just a shade too vigorously. Where we have light spilling over the scene directly from the floodlights, we can blank this excess out by strategically placed sheets of black cardboard, or with barndoors in case we use spotlights. If the offending light comes off the background, as it did in this case, then a remedy is more difficult to find. A properly used polarising filter would have solved the problem, as the angle of the hull in relation to the camera is just about right to allow this filter to work to its full capacity. Had the hull been sprayed matt, there would not have been any difficulty in the first place, because this is a clear case of direct reflection of a bright area in the background by a highly reflective part of the model. This incidentally, applies to a great many models; the shine of their finish is very often far too pronounced to help the realism we are trying to achieve. A complete matt-spray, on the other hand, isn't the answer either; the truth lies probably somewhere between full-gloss and semi-matt. The latter is sometimes still too dull and we have experimented with thin oil rubbed into a semi-gloss finish, which had encouraging results, also because the advantage of this treatment is that the effect is a slightly irregular and ultimately controllable shine. We can even wash it off again if we so desire. The trouble with most models is that they are just too neat and tidy to be real. The real problem with a very high gloss, we feel, is not so much the gloss itself, but the fact that the reflections that result, are out of scale, which is made worse by the fact that on many models fine details cannot be made to scale, or they would have to be far too thin and fragile; consequently they are too thick and sometimes even clumsy. Unfortunately these are the parts that catch the light in the first place and most of our reflections are on these tell-tale details. Since we are practically without exception interested only in taking photographs of our own models, it does pay to give some thought to all this when we are building them. For this very reason we hollowed out the exhaust stacks on the SPAD (pages 44-47, as well as the cover and centre-spread) and the muzzles of the anti-tank cannon of the Stuka (pages 64-68).

The author would like to conclude this excursion into the photographic world with stressing once again that there are virtually no limits to the illusions we can create in a properly set up table-top. You have been shown aircraft in positions that you might have considered impossible before. The principles applied can be easily put to work on, for instance, a car on a racing track. In a way, it is a pity this book is limited almost entirely to models of aeroplanes, with a few ships thrown in for good measure, but as explained, aircraft are definitely the most photogenic of scale models. We all have our preferences in this wide field of scale-modelling and we all know exactly how we would like to see our model in a picture.

Perhaps until now you have done little more than make a few attempts to photograph your favourite model in a more or less exciting situation and perhaps the results have been disappointing. If this is so, this book has been written especially for you, and we can only hope that we have removed any obstacles that have hitherto stopped you, and that you are now on your way to good model photographs.

R

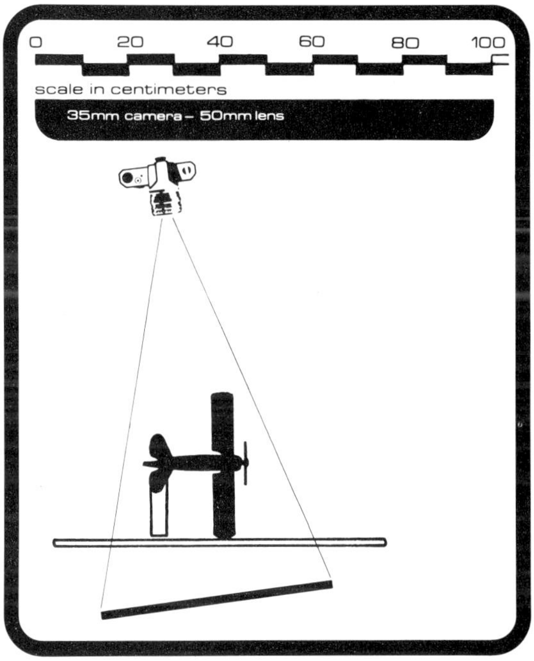

Because of the relatively high cost of colour prints, we have assumed that the average amateur photographer will not be so extravagant as to use such a print as background. We felt, however, that the appropriate place to afford ourselves such luxury would be the cover of this book, doubling as the centre-spread. To keep our expenses as low as possible, as well as to show how a similar thing could be realized by the readers, we determined beforehand the smallest size colour print that would still accomodate our model comfortably. Of course this is important in black and white photography too.

We set our table-top as in diagram **R**, but substitute the background with a plain sheet of paper, which we bring increasingly closer to the camera. No doubt there will come a moment at which the model will start throwing a shadow on this dummy background; by adjusting our mainlight a little we will find that we can come closer still. When the nearest setting is reached, we will have to find the four corners on the plain background that constitute the size of the colour print which will eventually replace it. Looking in the viewfinder of our SLR camera, we can move four small black squares or triangles, their 90° corners turned outward, round the estimated perimeter of the area and so ascertain the precise field of view. The next bigger print size will be the one to order; if, for instance, we find that our camera covers an area of 31 x 47cm, then the next commercial print size we would have to pay for would be 40 x 50cm, even if we only wanted the smaller area, so we may as well get the full size and have a few clouds to play with.

Make sure the print is matt; nothing reflects better than a glossy photographic print. Since the camera will look at it squarely, a polarising filter will have no effect whatsoever; we did use this filter with success, however, to cut back a few disturbing highlights along the fuselage top.

The longer the lens we use, the smaller the print can be, on account of the narrower field of view. All these factors have to be taken into account when it comes to keeping our costs down.

The author gratefully acknowledges the following people, who cheerfully lent him their precious models:

Rod Murdoch: figs. 34-36; 41-47; 64; 66-74.
Bill Bishop: figs. 1-9; 18-33; 65.
Bruce Usher: fig. 87.
Captain C.E.B. Carter, by courtesy of Mr. and Mrs. Zirkzee: fig. 88.